The Politics of State and City Administration

SUNY Series in Public Administration
in the 1980s

Peter Colby, Editor

The Politics of
State and City
Administration

Glenn Abney
and
Thomas P. Lauth

State University of New York Press

Published by
State University of New York Press, Albany

© 1986 State University of New York

Printed in the United States of America

For information, address State University of New York Press,
State University Plaza, Albany, N.Y., 12246

Library of Congress Cataloging in Publication Data

Abney, Glenn.
    The politics of state and city administration.

    (SUNY series in public administration in the 1980s)
    Includes index.
    1. State governments.   2. Municipal government--
United States.   3. Politics, Practical--United States.
I. Lauth, Thomas P.   II. Title.   III. Series.
JK2408.A26   1986   353.9   85-14873
ISBN 0-88706-255-5
ISBN 0-88706-256-3 (pbk.)

*For Frances Abney, Bill Abney,
Mary Lauth and the memory of
Thomas P. Lauth*

Contents

Tables   ix

Acknowledgments   xv

1. The Political Environment of State and
   City Administration   1

Part I. The Politics of State Administration

    A Brief Introduction to State Government .   18

2. The Tasks of State Administrators   21

3. The Governor as Chief Administrator   40

4. The Limits of Legislative Influence   63

5. Exchanges between Interest Groups and
   State Administrators   82

6. "Speaking Truth to Power" in the State
   Appropriations Process   106

Part II. The Politics of City Administration

    A Brief Introduction to City Government .   130

7. Reform and Rational Decision Making   132

8. Influence of the Chief Executive on
   City Line Agencies   154

9. Council Intervention in Municipal
   Administration   176

10. Interest Group Influence in City
    Policy Making 195

11. A Comparative Analysis of Service Distribution
    and Rule Enforcement Decisions in Cities 213

12. Conclusion 221

Notes 227

Index 253

Tables

2.1 Percentage Distribution of State   24
Administrators' Ranking of Departmental
Tasks

2.2 Percentage of State Administrators'   26
Ranking of Impact on Agency Programs
and Objectives by External Political Actors

2.3 Individual Administrators' Ranking of   31
Importance of Management Task by State's
Average Ranking

2.4 Percentage of Administrators' Primary Task   32
Choice According to Perceived Factors
Affecting State Legislature Appropriations

2.5 Percentage of State Administrators'   35
Ranking of External Political Actors'
Understanding of Departmental Policy Area

3.1 Agency Heads' Perceptions of Relative   42–43
Influence of Governor on Administrative
Departments by State

3.2 Gamma Correlation between State Agency   48
Heads' Ranking of Governor's Relative
Influence on Department and Governor's
Performance of Administrative Roles

3.3   Correlation between State Agency Heads'   51
      Ranking of Governor's Relative Influence on
      Departments and External Political Actors'
      Relative Understanding of Policy Area
      Problems

3.4   State Administrators' Average Discretion in   54
      Expenditures by Use of Legislative
      Committees

3.5   Percentage of State Agency Heads   57
      Responding to Governor's Influence by
      Governor's Criteria for Rewarding
      Departments

3.6   Percentages of State Agency Heads' Role   59
      Relations with Governor

4.1   Percentage of State Agency Heads Ranking   65
      of Legislature's and Governor's Relative
      Influence by Method of Selecting
      Department Heads

4.2   State Agency Heads' Ranking of   68
      Legislature's Influence by Percentage of
      Departmental Budget from Federal Funds

4.3   States Ranked by Average Degree of   70
      Department Heads' Lobbying of Legislature

4.4   Calls by Legislators on State Agency Heads   76
      in Regard to Constituents

5.1   Percentages of State Agency Heads   85
      Requesting Interest Group Resources

5.2   Percentages of State Agency Heads   86
      Reporting Requests for Departmental
      Resource by Interest Groups

5.3 Distribution of State Agency Heads by 87
Exchange Patterns with Interest Groups

5.4 Percentage of State Agency Heads in Each 89
Exchange Pattern According to Effects of
Interest Groups

5.5 Percentage of State Agency Heads in Each 91
Exchange Pattern According to Interest
Group Attributes Facilitating Interaction

5.6 Percentage of State Agency Types by 94–95
Exchange Types

5.7 States Ranked by Level of Interaction of 101–102
Departments in State with Interest Groups

6.1 Factors in State Executive Budget Office 113
Recommendations for State Agencies

6.2 Relationship of Effectiveness as Reason for 116
Governor's Agency Budget Increase to
Governor's Response to Interest Group
Lobbying and Legislative Support

6.3 Information of Most Interest to Legislatures 119
and Appropriations Committees in
Considering Agency Requests

6.4 Relationship of State Legislative Interest in 123
Agency Efficiency and Effectiveness to
Budget Changes for Constituent Benefit

7.1 City Manager and Mayoral Cities According 136
to At-large Elections and Political Party
Activity Level

7.2   Percentages of City Department Heads'   138
      Rankings of Departmental Objectives'
      Importance by Degree of Municipal Reform

7.3   Percentages of City Department Heads'   140
      Rankings of Departmental Objectives'
      Importance for City Chief Executive by
      Degree of Municipal Reform

7.4   Percentages of City Department Heads'   144
      Rankings of Six Factors' Importance in City
      Council Department Appropriations

7.5   Percentage of City Department Heads'   146
      Rankings of Five Factors' Importance in
      City Council Department Appropriations

7.6   Percentages of City Department Heads'   149
      Rankings of Departmental Objectives'
      Importance for City Chief Executive by
      Degree of Municipal Reform for Cities
      between 50,000 and 100,000

7.7   Percentages of City Department Heads'   150
      Rankings of Departmental Objectives'
      Importance for City Chief Executive by
      Degree of Municipal Reform in Three
      Western States

8.1   City Chief Executive Influence Index by   160
      Methods of Selecting Department Head

8.2   City Chief Executive Influence Index by   162
      Power to Remove Department Head

8.3   Reasons for Supporting City Chief   166
      Executive Influence Index by Department

8.4   City Chief Executive Influence Index by   168
      Reasons for Supporting Department

8.5   Combinations of Three City Chief Executive   170
      Relationships with Departments by
      Influence Index

8.6   City Chief Executive Influence Index by   172
      Discretion in Patterns of Sevice Delivery

8.7   City Chief Executive Influence Index by   174
      Reasons Department Heads Contacted
      Chief Executive

9.1   City Council Member Requests to City   178
      Departments

9.2   Types of City Council Members' Requests to   183
      City Departments by Degree of Municipal
      Reform

10.1 Extent of Interest Group Effects on Policy   197
      Reported by Various City Department
      Heads

10.2 Most Influential Interest Groups Reported   199
      by City Department Heads

10.3 Extent of Interest Group Effects on Policy   202
      as Reported by City Department Heads
      According to City Size

10.4 Interest Group Routes of Access Reported   203
      by Various City Department Heads

10.5 Correlations between City Interest Group   207
      Routes of Access and Influence of Interest
      Groups Reported by Various City
      Department Heads

11.1 Percentages of City Department Heads   215
      Citing Factors Important in Decisions
      About Service Distribution and Regulatory
      Enforcement

Acknowledgments

We incurred many debts during the preparation of this book. Most of them cannot be repaid, only gratefully acknowledged.

It would have been impossible to conduct our research on the politics of state and city administration without the cooperation of state agency and city department heads who took the time to respond to our surveys. We learned a great deal from them and appreciate their contribution to our research efforts.

Financial support for the surveys was provided by the Dean's Research Fund, College of Arts and Sciences, Georgia State University. Donald L. Fairchild made resources and staff of the Department of Political Science at Georgia State University available to us throughout the life of the project. We appreciate his generous support.

Deborah Barrow and Karen Mashke provided excellent research assistance during the early stages of the project. They better than anyone else know that this book was once a stack of questionnaires and coding sheets. Lucy Hayes turned drafts edited by two authors into clean manuscript with remarkable efficiency and good humor. We appreciate their efforts on our behalf.

Earlier versions of some of the chapters have appeared in academic journals. In those instances we profited from the advice and suggestions of anonymous reviewers. They contributed to this book without knowing it. We appreciate their help as well as that of the reviewers provided by the SUNY Press.

Two of our friends and colleagues have been especially helpful because of their continuing interest and constant encouragement — Howard Ball, University of Utah and Phillip Cooper, State University of New York at Albany.

Nancy and Jeannie have sustained us throughout, even conceding their living and dining rooms when we met to work on the manuscript. They are no doubt pleased that the work is done. We thank them for their love and support.

Responsibility for whatever shortcomings remain despite the efforts of others to save us from errors of fact or interpretation is, of course, ours alone.

Glenn Abney
Atlanta, GA

Thomas P. Lauth
Athens, GA

Chapter *1*

The Political Environment of State and City Administration

This book is about the politics of state and city administration in the United States. More specifically, it is about perceived interactions between state and city administrators and other participants in the political process who seek to influence state and city administration and upon whom administrators depend in order to carry out their responsibilities and achieve their objectives. Although some state and city administrators may prefer to think of themselves only as program managers or policy experts, governmental administration in a democratic society is carried out within a political environment that makes demands of as well as places constraints upon administrative actions. In the following chapters we analyze the relationship between state and city administrators and their respective political environments. This analysis is based primarily upon information obtained from national surveys of state and municipal government department heads. While administrators at all levels of state and city government from time to time have political encounters with those who seek to influence their actions, department heads are the officials who are most likely to have significant and recurring interactions with other political actors and institutions. Therefore, their perceptions of administrative interaction with the political environment are of central importance to understanding the politics of state and city administration.

I. Public Administration Is Different

It is the political nature of public administration that sets it apart from management in the private sector. There are, of course, many similarities between public and private sector management. Indeed, some would argue that management is essentially the same activity whether it is performed in the private sector or the public sector.[1] However, those who hold that view often fail to distinguish between the differences in purposes and objectives of public and of private organizations, on the one hand, and the similarity of their management processes on the other. Private-sector organizations are usually concerned with the delivery of a product or service for profit, while public-sector organizations are supposed to be concerned with the performance of services in response to either citizen demands or perceived citizen needs. The criteria by which their performance in achieving these differing organizational purposes and objectives is evaluated are also different. For private-sector organizations, the criteria are essentially economy and efficiency for the organization, i.e., the maximization of profit. For public-sector organizations, the goals of efficiency and economy are important, but the crucial considerations are responsiveness and accountability. In a democracy, those who occupy the positions of government are supposed to be answerable to the citizenry for their actions. The degree to which public organizations are responsive to the needs and demands of citizens, and the extent to which accountability is fixed on them for the quality of their performance, distinguishes them from private organizations. Although the management processes of public- and private-sector organizations have similarities, the differences in purposes of those organizations as well as differences in the criteria for evaluating their performance place different kinds of demands and constraints on managers in the public sector. In short, public administration is different from its private sector counterpart activity because of the importance of politics in determining the objectives and maintaining the accountability of administrative actions.

II. Administration and Politics: An Uneasy Relationship

The history of public administration in the United States, Herbert Kaufman has argued, can be seen as a continuous struggle to minimize the impact of narrow political interests on neutral professional competence in administration, while at the same time seeking to maximize the political responsiveness and accountability of administrators to the elected legislative and executive representatives of the people.[2]

Under the spoils system, the primary consideration for holding public office was partisan activity. The principal mechanism for attempting to check partisan intrusion into administration and increase the technical and professional competence of administrators has been the merit system of personnel selection and promotion. Although not all states and local governments have a merit selection process (except in those program areas where federal grant-in-aid requirements mandate it), nearly every state and many municipalities have a substantial portion of their work force covered by some sort of professional personnel system.

While efforts to limit partisan political influence in administration have been relatively successful, public administrators are nevertheless very much involved in the political process. Public administration is virtually inseparable from politics in two important ways. First, administrators are involved in the formulation and implementation of public policies. To the extent that administrative agencies are involved in program development and policy formulation, they are participants in the political process. And to the degree that they apply broadly articulated social rules to specific sets of circumstances — exercising discretion in the determination of how policies will be implemented — administrative agencies are also participating in political decision making.[3] Second, since administrators are involved in policy making, it is necessary in a democratic society for the legislative and executive representatives of the people to have supremacy over administrative institutions and actors. Responsiveness and accountability of administrators are attained through their interactions with legislators, the chief executive, interest groups, and officials at other levels of government. Public administration is inseparable from politics in that administrators develop, interpret, and implement policy, and other political actors seek to influence those policy decisions.

Administrators confront an apparent dilemma. Their professional norms of neutrality in implementation lead them to emphasize management and program development. Yet their program resources come from external political actors for whom neutrality is not likely to be an important value. How state administrators balance these apparently conflicting tasks of being neutral administrators while interacting successfully with external political actors is the subject of Chapter 2. Subsequent chapters also focus on how administrators perceive their relationships with external political actors.

III. The Political Actors

A. The Chief Executive

The chief executive is the one popularly elected official most directly charged with bringing about responsiveness and accountability in the executive branch. The executive reform movement at the state and local levels enhanced the formal powers of chief executives. When the chief executive possesses the full array of formal executive powers (direct control over the preparation and execution of the budget, the item veto, broadly defined appointment and removal powers, a minimal number of other elected executive branch officials with whom power must be shared, absence of legal prohibitions against reelection), his or her ability to govern is strengthened. However, the net effect of the executive reform movement has been mixed. For example, at the state level, gubernatorial budget powers have been widely strengthened in this century,[4] yet the number of independently elected department heads remains high.[5] Although victory in an election confers on a chief executive the authority to govern, his or her ability to govern is likely to depend very much on the skillfulness with which the state or local bureaucracy can be penetrated.

There are, however, limitations on the ability of the chief executive to exercise control over administrators. The ability of a governor or mayor and his or her political appointees to penetrate the bureaucracy is likely to be limited by its administrative expertise and professionalism. Administrative expertise within the bureaucracy can be a mixed blessing for a chief executive. On the one hand it means that political decisions "will be guided by competent technical advice and carried out by skilled personnel."[6] On the other hand, expertise increases the potential for administrators' preferences and values to prevail over the preferences and values of the chief executive. Administrative expertise in a bureaucracy is partially the result of having highly trained professionals who possess the skills needed by agencies in order to accomplish their program objectives. Francis Rourke notes that expertise also results from the practical knowledge that comes with experience. As administrators concentrate their attention on specific problems and continually perform their functions, they tend to develop experience-based expertise. One consequence of this development, Rourke points out, is the near-monopoly of information that comes with it[7] — an important source of agency power.

The ability of chief executives to exercise control over executive branch departments is also limited by the opportunity that administrators may have to exercise discretion in program implementation. Discretion is exercised in interpreting legislative intent and applying it to particular rule enforcement or service delivery situations. Often the ability of a legislature or city council to arrive at consensus on important policy questions is facilitated by agreements to delegate to administrators the responsibility for making judgments about specific policy applications that would be potentially divisive for the legislature or council. Initially, agencies refine policies formulated by the legislative body and produce a framework for implementing them by "the drafting and adopting of rules and regulations that define further the intent of the policy and guide administrators in its eventual application to specific cases and programs."[8] From the perspective of the chief executive, administrative discretion, like professional expertise, may be a double-edged sword. It is functional in that agency personnel have the flexibility to accommodate unanticipated situations and individualize policy applications to meet the needs of particular constituencies. On the other hand, whenever administrative actions alter the intent of policies established by the legislative body or the interpretation of those policies advocated by the chief executive, discretion may be dysfunctional for them.

Chapter 3 discusses the role of the American state governor as chief administrator. In that chapter, gubernatorial influence is said to be evident whenever state government department heads take the governor's policy position into account when they make their own decisions, and whenever governors have more impact on state agency decisions than other political actors seeking to influence those decisions. Although governors are nominally the chief administrative officers of state government, they do not dominate state administration. They appear to be more comfortable with the routine role of program manager than with the more proactive role of policy leader.

Chapter 8 assesses the ability of U.S. municipal chief executives (mayors and city managers) to intervene in the administrative process. In essence, the chapter asks what makes a chief executive capable of penetrating bureaucratic routines. Aspects of formal power and personal style are investigated. While this chapter demonstrates what counts in penetrating the bureaucracy, it also indicates the triumph of professionalism in administration over political control. City chief executives tend to defer to administrative professionals.

B. *The Legislature*

Legislative bodies seek to influence executive branch agencies in a number of important ways: by providing a statutory and organizational basis for their existence, through periodic program authorization and oversight investigations, and by annual (biennial in some states) appropriations. Although legislative bodies are the primary institutions for achieving popular control over governmental administration, state legislatures and city councils are somewhat better suited for the periodic review of administrative actions than they are for the direction and coordination of ongoing administrative activities. Even though state government department heads perceive the legislature to have a great deal of impact upon them, they also perceive the legislature to have a relatively low level of understanding about their programs and needs. This is partially explained by the different perspectives, value systems, and needs of state administrators and state legislators.

In addition to institutional interactions with the state legislature or city council, state and municipal executive branch agencies frequently have exchanges with individual legislators or members of the city council over such matters as constituency case work and the agency's search for legislative support for its program needs. An individual legislator or council member may from time to time contact an executive department on behalf of a constituent who is dissatisfied with the treatment he or she has received as a client of the department, or they may request information for a constituent regarding eligibility for services provided by the department. On other occasions legislators may make contact seeking to influence an administrative decision regarding rule enforcement or patterns of service delivery. They may also contact departments with requests for jobs for constituents or preferential treatment in the awarding of government contracts. The electoral advantages of constituency casework for legislators or council members are obvious. Appreciative constituents are expected to offer their electoral support for those representatives who intervened with the bureaucracy on their behalf. The principal danger associated with such intervention is that it may result in a violation of administrative "neutrality" by requiring administrators to provide special treatment for certain clients. Chapter 9 examines the extent to which constituent casework leads to intervention by city council representatives in municipal administration. Councilmember intervention is identified there as being of three kinds: informant, mediator, and procurer. Although council members' intervention continues despite the efforts of the municipal and executive reform movements, reform institutions have nevertheless been successful in structuring the patterns of intervention in such a manner as to preserve the "informational" purposes of intervention without significantly threatening the reform goal of "neutrality" in municipal administration.

While administrators may tend to view legislative inquiries as a nuisance, at least two advantages may accrue to agencies in the process. Legislative inquiries bring to the attention of agencies potential service delivery problems that may be developing with their personnel or procedures. Agencies can use responding to a casework inquiry as an occasion to inform legislators or council members about their programs.

Although the formal dependence of executive branch agencies on the state legislature or city council facilitates legislative control over administration, agencies are likely to establish other bases of political power that make them less susceptible to legislative control. Chapter 4 considers the limits of legislative influence. Although the state legislature has more influence over state administration than any other external actor, there are limits to the influence even of state legislatures. The ability of agency heads to use such allies as interest groups and federal and local administrators to reduce the influence of the legislature is discussed in that chapter.

C. Interest Groups

Although legislative and elected executive officials are the principal agents of political control of public bureaucracies, interest groups may also seek to influence the policies of state and city administrative agencies. A political interest group is a collection of individuals sharing a set of common attitudes which competes with other groups and makes demands upon government for benefits desired by its members.[9] Although interest group activity is sometimes viewed as problematic, it can also be regarded as a complementary form of popular participation in political decision making.

Executive branch agencies often develop relationships with clientele groups that they serve or regulate.[10] Such groups may make demands of the agency, but they can also be an important source of agency power[11] in dealing with other actors in the governmental process such as the chief executive, the legislature, other state agencies, or officials at other levels of government.

In Chapter 5 the relationship between interest groups and state government departments is conceptualized as interactive and reciprocal rather than one in which departments are viewed as passively responding to interest group initiatives in the policy process. Interest groups are not perceived by state agency heads as harmful; rather, they are viewed as providing state agencies with valuable resources. Each set of participants in the policy process needs the resources possessed by the other. Mutually dependent agencies and interest groups benefit most from their exchanges. Departments having a narrow policy concern have closer relationships with groups than departments with broader policy concerns. Such groups apparently are capable of reducing the influence of the governor and legislature over selected aspects of state administration, but not in subverting their control entirely.

Chapter 10 reports that municipal department heads perceive interest groups to be important in the formulation of public policy, albeit less significant than chief executives and city councils. The access route chosen by interest groups — through the city council, the chief executive, or the department — is reported to affect group influence. Most municipal department heads perceive the activities of interest groups as benign, but when it comes indirectly through the city council they are likely to regard such influence on their policy decisions as threatening their administrative neutrality.

D. The Judiciary

Most discussions of government begin with an explanation of the three branches of government. Yet judges and courts are not usually significant external actors for state and city administrators.[12] Their relationships with courts are often handled through intermediaries such as state and city legal departments. Furthermore, the independent nature of judicial institutions limits their interaction with administrators. Occasionally, court decisions may have far-reaching consequences for policy and its implementation. In a few states court-ordered improvements in correction and mental health facilities have required substantial increases in funding and brought the court and state agency into a continuing relationship during the period in which the court monitored agency compliance with its orders.[13] In general, however, the consequences of court decisions are less regular and sustained than consequences that flow from administrative relationships with other political actors. For these reasons, our focus is on the interaction of state and city administrators with chief executives, legislative bodies, and interest groups.

III. The Lost World of State and City Administration

Nearly thirty years ago an often cited article argued that students of government had neglected the world of municipal government.[14] Today, a similar conclusion could be reached about the world of state and city administration. Students of public administration are taught about administration at the national level, but considerably less attention is given to either state or municipal administration. Yet, in terms of numbers of employees and in terms of where the bulk of domestic program money is ultimately spent, governmental administration in the United States is primarily state and local.

Because state governments, as well as city governments, differ from each other, students of administration are able to study them on a comparative basis. For example, the fact that some chief executives have stronger formal powers than others affords the opportunity to study the effects of such powers on the chief executive's ability to control agencies of the executive branch.

While states and cities each differ among themselves, there are certain qualities which make each level unique. For example, cities differ from the states because of the enormous efforts in this century to remove politics from government. More than at any other level of government, the goal has been to make city government into a rational enterprise. In particular, the municipal reform movement sought to professionalize city governments as a way of reducing the influence of partisanship in municipal policy making. The reform movement was aimed at increasing efficiency, effectiveness, and equity in urban administration — in short, making administration more rational. The most important structural changes associated with this objective were: the establishment of a professional chief executive (city manager), the use of nonpartisan elections to reduce the influence of political parties, and the use of at-large elections to discourage pork barrel activities in city councils. The effects of this movement on city administration are profound, and the chapters of this book shed significant light on those effects.

In Chapter 7, for example, evidence is presented which indicates that the municipal reform movement and its institutions appear to have made a difference in the attitudes and behavior of city officials. Administrators in reformed cities are found to differ from administrators in nonreformed cities in their service delivery goals. Administrators from the most fully reformed cities were more likely than administrators from the most absolutely nonreformed cities to espouse the goals of efficiency, effectiveness, and equity in service delivery. The effects of the reform movement are explored in every chapter of the section on city administration, including Chapter Eleven's discussion of distributional and enforcement decisions made by city administrators. That chapter shows administrators to have much discretion. They are decision makers. The question addressed here is how they use that discretion. Are public service decisions keyed to technical criteria and professional values, or are they controlled by elected officials? The likelihood that city government department heads will consider requests from council members and the policy positions of the chief executive during the course of making service distribution and rule enforcement decisions appears to be related to political culture. Those department heads who report considering the position of the chief executive in their decisions are also the ones most likely to report considering requests from council members. Interest groups also appear to be more active in those cities. Thus, it appears that an environment of political competition over policy encourages administrative decision makers to pay more attention to the views of elected decision makers. While administrative decisions in city departments seem to be based primarily upon neutral criteria, as the current literature contends,[15] those decisions are not immune from intervention by external political actors.

State administration differs from city government because the influence of the legislative branch is stronger in state administration than at any other level of government. The executive at the city and national levels has emerged as the stronger branch of government. While executives have gained in influence at the state level, their dominance is far from established. Many key department heads are still elected or appointed by boards. In this environment of potential legislative and group intervention in administration, significant questions of administrative neutrality and responsible policy making are raised.

Chapter 6, for example, reports the perceptions of state administrators regarding their own behavior and that of other participants in the state budgetary process. Administrators are generally regarded as having different sets of values than elected officials. Elected officials are said to pursue distributive benefits for constituents and to evaluate programs on the basis of inputs (how much money is spent on districts or programs) rather than outputs or outcomes. Administrators are said to be more "rational." Their values are those of efficiency, effectiveness, and neutrality. This chapter raises the question of how much rationality there is in the allocation of state financial resources. Does it do any good to speak "truth" to the political decision makers? In the quest for state appropriations, rational decision-making criteria are seen to be only moderately important to budget makers, including state administrators. Further, rational values appear to be less influential in state policy making than they are in cities that have the institutions of the reform movement.

IV. Objectives and Methods

This study of administrative politics is essentially about calls for professional neutrality and demands for political control in state and municipal governments. Most textbooks in public administration and on state and local government neglect this topic or deal with it only superficially. This is due in large measure to a dearth of systematic and reliable information on the subject. More than a decade ago Ira Sharkansky[16] pointed out that the behavioral movement in political science had ignored the agencies of state government, and Douglas Fox[17] noted the paucity of literature dealing with state and local bureaucracy. Malcolm Jewell's call in 1982[18] for comparative research in state government suggests that the condition which Sharkansky and Fox described continues to exist. Because the work presented in the following chapters is empirical, comparative, and subnational in focus, it should help reduce the deficiency which Sharkansky, Fox, and Jewell identified.

State government data, with the exception of those reported in Chapter 6, were obtained from a mail survey of department heads in the fifty states. Out of a total population of 1,119 state government department heads, 70 percent (778) responded to the survey. All fifty states are represented, no state having a response rate of lesss than 54 percent. The survey covered heads of agencies designated by the states as "departments." Also included were the heads of substantive units organized as independent agencies, e.g., commissions and boards. Excluded were the staff agencies such as planning, budgeting, and personnel, as well as any other agency included within the executive office of the governor.

The data reported in Chapter 6 were obtained from mail surveys of state executive and legislative budget officers. Returns were received from forty-eight executive budget officers (96 percent of the population) and 45 legislative budget officers (90 percent of the population). In those instances where a state did not have a legislative budget officer, the chief staff member of the House Appropriations Committee was included in the survey.

Municipal government data were obtained from a mail survey of police, fire, and public works department heads in all cities in the United States with a population of 50,000 or more.[19] Those cities were found in forty-seven states and the District of Columbia. Although police, fire and public works are not the only line agencies found in cities, they are the departments most commonly found in all cities.[20] For that reason the survey was limited to those departments. Returns were received from 56 percent of the survey population — 238 fire chiefs (37 percent of the total response), 227 public works department heads (35 percent of the total), and 181 police chiefs (28 percent of the total). In our analysis we weighted the responses from public works directors and fire chiefs so as to equalize the number of respondents in those categories with the number of responses from heads of police departments. Since preliminary analysis of the data revealed only slight differences in the perceptions of the three types of administrators, weighting was utilized to allow us to focus on variables other than administrative type in attempting to explain variation in administrative decision patterns. As a result of the weighting, the population was decreased to 543 from 646.

The returns tended to be quite reflective of the population. For example, 44 percent of the returns were from cities of 100,000 or more, while 40 percent of the cities included in the survey were of that size. Similarly, 53 percent of the cities in the population had a council–manager form of government compared to 58 percent of the respondents in the sample. The response rate did, however, vary somewhat by region (as defined by U.S. Bureau of the Census). The response rate from cities in Western states was 61 percent, in Southern states 60 percent, in North Central states 51 percent, and in Northeastern states 37 percent. Even though the response rate from cities in Northeastern states deviates the most from the overall survey response rate, returns from that region are representative by city type. For example, 22 percent of the regional survey population was from city manager cities and 22 percent of the Northeastern respondents were also from city manager cities. In general, regional or state variations in response rate do not appear to affect the results of our analysis.[21]

Chapters 2 through 6 examine the politics of administration within state political systems, and Chapters 7 through 11 deal with administrative politics in municipal political systems.

Part **I**

The Politics of
State Administration

A Brief Introduction
to State Government

Historically, the legislature has been more significant for U.S. state administrators than has been the governor. Distrust of the British monarch led to the institution of a weak governor in the constitutions of the American states. But in the last fifty years the powers of governors have been significantly increased. Reorganization of state executive branches has consolidated and realigned agencies so as to increase the span of control of governors over their administrative apparatus. As a result of increases in their formal powers, governors in most states now can propose an executive budget, administer the budget passed by the legislature, and appoint and remove the heads of a number of state agencies. Nevertheless, in some respects most executive branches still fit the weak executive model. A number of departments are still headed by elected executives or by boards rather than by single appointees of the governor. For example, the chief legal officer of state government, the attorney general, is appointed by the governor in only four states.

While the executive reform movement worked to increase governors' control over administration, the civil service reforms of this century and the increasing role of professionalism in administration have served to enlarge the countervailing independence of state administrators. Although many department heads are now appointed and removed by the governor, most state employees are protected by law from removal for political reasons. Furthermore, the complexity of state services requires administrators with professional skills. Thus, the ability of governors to use job patronage to reward supporters is limited.

Although legislatures have been considered the dominant branch of state government, in recent years critics have condemned state assemblies for their amateurism and poor performance. Critics note that legislatures have been slow to modernize. For example, state assemblies failed to reapportion their districts as their state populations changed from rural to urban. Not until *Baker versus Carr* in 1962 did state legislatures begin to apportion their election districts to reflect population changes. State assemblies are criticized also for their lack of institutional staff, their part-time nature, and lack of staff support for their individual members. Of course, in the past thirty years, legislatures have improved on many of these points. In 1952, 38 of the 48 states legislatures were in session only every other year. By 1982 only 9 state assemblies met biennially. Nevertheless, many of the criticisms of state legislatures are still applicable. The lack of expertise possessed by state legislators increases the influence of lobbyists for interest groups and state agencies.

In the politics of state administration, elected legislative and executive branch officials seek to direct and control agencies of the executive branch which have responsibility for delivering the services and administering the regulatory activities of state government. The relationship between administrators and elected officials is characterized by cooperation and conflict. Agencies need elected officials to authorize and sustain their activities. From time to time they also rely on the political strength of one of the elected branches to support and protect them in their dealings with either the other branch or with interest groups which seek to influence their activities. Elected officials rely on the expertise of agencies in the formulation of policy decisions and in the execution of state government programs. Despite the many incentives for elected and administrative officials to cooperate with each other, their relationship is also characterized by conflict. The policy goals of the governor and the program objectives of individual legislators are sometimes in conflict with the organizational or professional values of state administrators. When professional and organizational values are strongly held, the hierarchical authority of formal bureaucratic organizations may not be sufficient to enable elected leaders to direct and control state administrators without a struggle.

In the following chapters we present evidence which enhances our understanding of the conflict and cooperation that characterize the politics of administration in the United States.

Chapter *2*

The Tasks of State Administrators: Internal Management or External Relations

Public administrators are individuals who must carry out two distinct, but not unrelated, sets of responsibilities. First, they have management responsibilities which entail the development and implementation of programs. Second, they must appeal to political actors who are external to their agency (legislators, the chief executive, interest groups, and officials at other levels of government) in order to obtain the resources necessary to continue existing programs and develop new ones. As Eugene Bardach reminded us, success in implementing public policies involves more than efficient management, it also requires that other actors in the policy process be induced to contribute resources over which they have control so that agency programs may be continued or developed.[1] Thus, public administrators, particularly the heads of executive branch agencies, must perform two essential tasks: management and external relations. This chapter investigates the relative importance of these tasks to state agency heads and discusses some of the causes and consequences of the patterns identified.

Research Questions

Early in this century the good government reform movement sought to separate administration from politics — particularly from partisanship and patronage politics.[2] Reliance upon independent boards and commissions to set public policies, the use of civil service systems for the selection and promotion of public employees, and emphasis upon expertise and scientific management were manifestations of the efforts to separate administration from politics. In its contemporary form, this view of administration emphasizes professionalism in the public service and noninterference by external actors in agency activities. The degree to which this model of administration exists in the United States is reflected in the difficulties which chief executives experience in penetrating the bureaucracy,[3] as well as in those which legislators experience in attempting to achieve effective oversight of administration.[4]

However, efforts to insulate administration from the dysfunctions of partisan politics and patronage were not intended to make administration insensitive to the directives of external political actors and unaccountable to their authority. Because policy implementation is often a form of policy making, insulation of administration carries with it the risk that important public issues will be decided by those who are unaccountable to the electorate and largely unaccountable to elected officials. When administration is performed in a closed system, agency programs and activities may be immune from the leadership of the chief executive or unresponsive to the needs of agency clients.

To what extent do public administrators separate themselves from the influence of external political actors? The literature reports many instances of separation between politics and administration. For example, the literature on urban service delivery indicates that rational, technical criteria tend to prevail over political considerations in decision making by administrators.[5] However, that literature also suggests that administrators are not immune from

the influence of external actors.[6] Program authorizations
and the resources necessary for program implementation
are still in the hands of external actors. Thus, Douglas
Arnold argues that federal program administrators decide
upon grant applications with an eye toward meeting the
electoral needs of congressmen.[7] Administrators must
induce external actors to continue to provide resources for
agency programs and activities. As long as such
dependence exists, the concerns of public administrators
must extend beyond internal agency management. The
first research objective of this chapter is to determine the
relative importance for state level administrators of the
tasks of internal management and program development
as against external relations.

Our second objective is to investigate the reasons why
some departments find external liaison a more important
task than do other agencies. Where external actors make
few demands of agencies, administrators may not need to
be as concerned with external liaison. Agencies which
have a substantial proportion of their work force covered
by civil service systems may be better able to resist
penetration by external actors. Furthermore, departments
run by boards rather than appointed executives may be
more able to concentrate on internal affairs.

The third objective is to determine if task choice
affects the nature of administrative behavior. According to
those advocating the separation of politics and administration, the dichotomy was supposed to produce more
efficient and effective delivery of public services. These
achievements were expected to occur because patronage
would no longer be a characteristic of administration. Program implementation would be based on rational and
technical criteria rather than concern for the wishes of
external actors.

Task Preferences

To determine the tasks of state administrators, we
have utilized our mail survey of the heads of administra-

tive departments described in Chapter 1. Respondents were asked to rank five tasks according to their importance for accomplishing agency objectives. These tasks included two (management and program development) i..ternal to the department. In the literature on public administration, the management task generally refers to concern about the routines (personnel, budgeting, and service delivery) of program implementation while program development refers to emphasis on adaptation, innovation and evaluation of outcomes. The other three tasks involve interaction with three sets of actors (the governor and the legislature, interest groups, and administrators at the federal and local levels) external to the department.

State agency heads tend to perceive their internal jobs of management and program development as more important for accomplishing their objectives than they do the tasks of relating to external actors. As indicated in Table 2.1, three-quarters of the respondents ranked one of the

Table 2.1. Percentage Distribution of State Administrators' Ranking of Departmental Tasks

	Ranking				
	First	Second	Third	Fourth	Fifth
Internal Tasks					
Management	55%	23%	9%	5%	2%
Program development	23	32	18	14	6
External Tasks					
Liaison with legislature and governor	13	27	34	14	5
Liaison with administrators at federal and local levels	3	8	19	28	33
Interest-group liaison	2	5	12	30	43

Note: Not all respondents ranked each task. Percentages for each task are calculated on the basis of all respondents (N = 778).

internal tasks (management or program development) as the most important in accomplishing the objectives of their agency. Over half of the administrators perceived management as their most important task. Only thirteen percent of the respondents perceived gubernatorial and legislative liaison as their most significant task. Because agency heads are probably more likely than other administrators to be concerned with this form of liaison, these data provide a strong argument for describing state administrators as primarily managers. A total of only five percent of the respondents cited liaison with interest groups or administrators at the federal or local levels as their primary tasks.

Although state administrators perceive internal tasks as more important than external relations for the accomplishment of agency objectives, state administrators are not independent of external actors. Indeed, two-fifths of the administrators perceived liaison with the governor and the legislature to be either first or second in importance of the tasks listed in Table 2.1. Furthermore, because administrators ranked internal tasks ahead of external relations does not mean that the external actors are not significant; internal concerns are perceived merely to be relatively more important.

Although the governor is a full-time official, and theoretically head of the administrative branch of government, it is the legislature which state administrators perceive as having the most impact on their agencies. However, there is not a great deal of difference between the impact of the governors and the legislature; as indicated in Table 2.2, 43 percent of the respondents perceived the legislature and 38 percent saw the governor as having the greatest impact on their agencies. The influence of the other actors was perceived to be considerably less than that of either the legislature or the governor. Only 6 percent cited federal administrators and 2 percent identified local administrators as having the greatest impact. Six percent perceived Congress and the President as most influential, and only 3 administrators cited locally elected

Table 2.2. Percentage of State Administrator's Ranking of Impact on Agency Programs and Objectives by External Political Actors

	First	Second	Third	Ranking Fourth	Fifth	Sixth	Seventh
External Political Actors							
Legislature	43%	33%	9%	9%	1%	1%	1%
Governor	38	33	13	6	4	1	1
Federal administrators	6	9	19	21	10	13	9
Congress and President	6	5	14	14	13	12	19
Interest groups	4	6	19	16	18	13	14
Local administrators	2	4	9	13	22	20	10
Locally elected officials	0*	3	10	13	15	19	22

Note: Not all respondents ranked each actor. Percentages for each political actor are calculated on the basis of all respondents (N = 778).

*Less than 0.5 percent.

officials as having the greatest impact. The external political environment of state agency heads would seem to be composed primarily of the legislature and the governor.

Choice of Tasks

On what bases do state administrators make their task choices? In particular, why might an administrator choose an internal task orientation over an external one? In this section, we shall investigate several factors thought to be relevant to the choices made by the respondents.

A. Departmental Characteristics

The choice of an internal task orientation over an external one might seem to be related to the nature of the state agencies and their personnel. Agencies pursuing internal tasks might be expected to be more professional than agencies pursuing external tasks. Presumably, the professional agency would be more likely to shun interaction with external actors. One measure of professionalism is the presence of a civil service system. Most of the department heads in this study reported that a large percentage of their employees are covered by a civil service system. In fact, 56 percent reported ninety-five percent or more of their agency's employees were so classified. However, contrary to our expectations, we found agencies pursuing internal tasks to be no more prone to the use of civil service than those pursuing external tasks. For example, only 49 percent of those agencies pursuing program development as a primary task reported having ninety-five percent or more of their employees under civil service, as compared with 55 percent of those pursuing gubernatorial and legislative liaison. Fifty-nine percent of the agencies pursuing management as a primary task reported this percentage of civil service employees. The use of state civil service appears relatively unrelated to task choice.

While task choice is unrelated to methods of choosing the personnel of state agencies, it is related to the mode of appointment of the agency head. Fifty-two percent of the heads (n = 169) appointed by the governor and approved by the legislature ranked gubernatorial and legislative liaison as a primary or secondary task compared with 38 percent of those respondents (n = 77) elected to their office and 41 percent of those (n = 148) appointed by boards. Clearly, where the selection process increases the dependence of state agency heads on external actors, the result is to increase the importance of external actors for agency heads.

While the selection process may encourage a greater responsiveness to the appointing official(s), professional education does not have the counter effect of insulating state agency heads. Agency heads who earned professional or graduate degrees are not more likely than other agency heads to pursue internal tasks. Most of the agency heads included in this study had a college degree (95 percent of the respondents) and many had graduate work or degrees (68 percent). The failure of education to account for variance in task orientation may be partially explained by the absence of the less educated in the ranks of agency heads. Apparently a prerequisite for appointment for most such state positions is a college degree.

The choice of tasks appears to be largely unrelated to state agency policy function. Although some types of agencies are more prone to internal tasks, uniformity rather than differences among the types of agencies is the pattern. Variations which exist among the agencies tend to be more a matter of choices between the internal tasks or among the external tasks, rather than a choice between internal tasks and external tasks. For example, even though heads of defense agencies (National Guard or state militia) tend to choose the task of liaison with other governmental administrators over the other two external tasks, they are no less committed to internal task choices than other agencies. Heads of state defense agencies do place less emphasis on liaison with the governor, legislature, and interest groups than do other respondents.

Choice between internal tasks by various policy types seems to be affected by personnel requirements. State agencies having a large number of workers, such as Departments of Public Safety, Human Services, or Mental Health, place a higher degree of emphasis on management than do other departments. On the other hand, agencies such as those dealing with law, industry, and trade tend to emphasize program development over management.

B. *Departmental Environment*

The internal characteristics of state government departments tend to have only a minor effect on task choice. Task selection appears to be more a product of the environment and its effect on agencies. A major component of the environment of any agency is the state in which it is located. Research has often indicated variation among the states in policy and administration.[8] Examination of task choice of agency heads by state indicates much variation. However, this examination does not reveal any relationship between task choice and such traditional variables as party competition or political culture. Consider the ten states where management ranks highest in importance: Indiana, Nebraska, Oregon, Kentucky, Louisiana, Florida, South Dakota, Pennsylvania, Iowa, and Arkansas. These states represent a wide variety of political culture and party competition.

Although the state rankings on internal tasks are not easily explained by traditional variables, variation on external tasks does conform to expectations. Oregon, a state known for significant interest group activity, ranks third among the fifty states in the significance of interest group liaison for agency heads. States where gubernatorial and legislative liaison ranks high for agency heads include New York, Michigan, Colorado, and Alaska. These states are known for their strong governors and/or active legislatures.[9] Even so, states with professional legislatures such as California and states having governors with strong formal powers such as New Jersey are not among the ten states where gubernatorial and legislative liaison is of greatest importance. Of course, that New Jersey and California do not rank so high on this task does not mean it is not an important task in these states, but only that other tasks are relatively more important.

Though the states do not necessarily conform to predictions from previous research, state variation is important in explaining task choice by individual agency heads. As can be seen in Table 2.3, the ranking of the states according to their administrators' average ranking of the significance of the management task is a good predictor of individual task decisions. For example, knowing that an agency head comes from Indiana (which ranks first among the states in administrators' ranking of the management task), we could predict management as the primary task choice of an agency head and be correct 71 percent of the time. A similar prediction for agency heads from New Mexico, which ranked last on management as a task choice, would be correct only 26 percent of the time. Use of other task choices by states serve equally well in predicting individual decisions. For example, 46 percent of the department heads in the state highest on gubernatorial and legislative liaison (Michigan) cited that task choice compared to none in the state (Massachusetts) lowest on that task choice. The external environment of a department (here represented by each state's administrators' average rankings) appears to be a better predictor of task choice than the internal characteristics of departments. Other illustrations of how this is so and what factors within a state affect task choice are considered below.

The activities of external actors clearly have a marked effect on task choice. Where state administrators report the governor to have a major impact on their appropriations from the legislature, the tendency is for them to be less prone to identify internal tasks as being of primary importance. We asked the respondents to rank seven factors as to their importance in affecting their department's appropriations from the legislature. Note that in Table 2.4 respondents identifying management and program devel-

Table 2.3. Individual Administrators' Ranking of Importance of Management Task by State's Average Ranking

	State's Average Ranking of Management Task		
	(16 states) Least important *(n=239)*	*(18 states)* In between importance *(n=249)*	*(16 states)* Most important *(n=239)*
Individual Administrators' Ranking of Management Task			
Most Important Task	28%	16%	9%
Second Most Important	26	24	23
Unimportant*	46	61	68
	100%	101%	100%

Note: State rankings were determined by averaging rankings of depart-ment heads from each state in regard to the management task.

Chi square is 34.91, with a probability of less than .01.

Percentages do not always total 100% due to rounding.

*Ranked as third, fourth, or fifth most important task. See Table 2.1.

opment as primary tasks are much less likely than those having the gubernatorial and legislative liaison task as their first concern to perceive the governor as an impor-tant determinant of their legislative appropriation. Iden-tification with internal tasks appears inversely related to the strength and resources of external actors.

The impact of external actors can be seen through the following examples. For those state administrators (n=119) identifying interest group liaison as one of their three most important tasks, 30 percent identified interest group activity as one of the three most significant factors affecting legislative appropriations for their agencies, com-pared to only 14 percent of the other (n=458) respondents ranking this task. Similarly, of those (n=71) ranking

Table 2.4. Percentage of Administrators' Primary Task Choice According to Perceived Factors Affecting State Legislature Appropriations

	Department Heads' Primary Task		
Most Important Appropriations Factor*	Management (n=372)	Program development (n=149)	Gubernatorial and legislative liaison (n=90)
Governor (1st)	34%	26%	50%
Level of state revenue (1st)	38	32	36
Objective measures of need (1st or 2nd)	30	38	18
Achievements of the departments (1st or 2nd)	29	38	19

*Other factors ranked by respondents were: lobbying by interest groups, lobbying by the department, and electoral needs of legislators.

interest groups as having the first or second most impact on their agencies (see Table 2.2), 55 percent cited interest group liaison as among their three most important tasks, compared to 16 percent of the other agency heads (n=590).

A similar point can be made about the impact of federal and local administrators on state agency heads. Money is a major resource under the control of federal administrators, which enables them to have an impact upon state agencies. The importance of the task of liaison with such outside administrators increases significantly with the importance of federal aid to the state department heads. Seventy percent of those (n=209) ranking liaison with administrators at other levels of government as one of their three most important tasks reported ten percent or more of their agency's budget to be composed of federal funds. Only 39 percent of the other state administrators (n = 441) reported a similar level of federal funding. Federal funding increases the significance of intergovernmental liaison.[10]

The relative unimportance of external tasks for state administrators is related to the low impact of external actors as influences on state agencies. We asked the respondents to indicate from a list provided them which things had been asked of them by the governor during the year preceding the survey. From this list, a cumulative index of governor's requests was created. As the number of governor's requests increases, so does the importance of gubernatorial and legislative liaison for state administrators.[11]

Not only does the degree of activity on the part of external actors affect state administrators' task choice, but so does the nature of that activity. Considering once again the data on Table 2.4, agency heads who perceive their appropriation from the legislature to be based on such criteria as the state's objective needs and the agency's achievements are more likely to be oriented toward the internal tasks of management and program development. The latter task selection is especially related to such criteria. State agency heads perceiving their agencies as being rewarded for good work or usefullness are more likely to place emphasis on internal tasks.

Another determinant in the environment of state agencies which affects task choices is perception by agency heads of how well external actors understand the agency and its programs. Administrators tend to have liaison with external actors who are supportive, and they tend to avoid contact with external actors who are perceived as failing to understand their problems.[12] To examine this relationship, we need to explore respondent perceptions of the level of understanding of the agency by external actors.

Although the data in Table 2.2 indicate the legislature to be perceived as having the most impact of all external actors, the data in Table 2.5 indicate that department heads do not perceive legislatures to be very understanding of policy. In fact, four other sets of external actors were ranked ahead of legislators as best understanding agency policies. However, almost a third of the respondents ranked the legislature as the second most understanding of their agency's policy area. In coping with the external environment, clearly administrators have difficulty with legislators. Their dilemma is that legislatures are perceived to have more impact on them than any other external actor, but comparatively less understanding. In contrast, of the various external actors, it is governors who are most likely to be perceived as most understanding of agency programs.

State administrators who place a high priority on liaison with external actors also tend to perceive those actors as having an understanding of their agencies. For example, of those respondents ranking gubernatorial and legislative liaison as their primary task (n = 99), 47 percent ranked the governor as the most understanding of the external actors, compared to 30 percent of those (n = 125) who ranked such liaison as their least or next to least significant task. Fifty-three percent of those ranking gubernatorial and legislative liaison as their most important task ranked the legislature as the first or second most understanding actor, compared to 36 percent of those ranking the gubernatorial and legislative task as their least or next to least important task. Those administrators who most lobby the legislature perceive the legislature as understanding them. For example, 58 percent of those administrators (n = 88) ranking the legislature as the most understanding actor described their lobbying as very active, compared to a similar level of lobbying by only 43 percent of the other (n = 643) respondents ranking the legislature.

Examination of the behavior of other external actors produces even more dramatic evidence of the relationship between understanding and liaison. Of those (n = 95) state administrators ranking interest groups as the most

Table 2.5. Percentage of State Administrators' Ranking of External Political Actors' Understanding of Departmental Policy Area

External Political Actor	First	Second	Third	Ranking Fourth	Fifth	Sixth	Seventh
Governor	40%	22%	14%	10%	6%	2%	2%
Federal administrators	16	11	15	12	10	24	5
Local administrators	15	11	12	18	14	7	4
Interest groups	12	12	15	14	15	11	10
Legislature	11	32	22	16	9	2	3
Locally elected officials	2	6	10	10	15	22	17
Congress and President	1	2	4	6	10	19	38

Note: Not all respondents ranked each actor. Percentages for each political actor are calculated on the basis of all respondents (N=778).

understanding external actor, 48 percent ranked interest group liaison as one of their three most important tasks, compared to a similar ranking by only 14 percent of the other (n=599) respondents ranking interest groups. As already indicated, department heads tend to avoid liaison with actors who they believe do not understand them. Two reasons can be suggested for this behavior. External actors change with their shifting electoral and political fortunes; administrators can wait for a change. Secondly, administrators may believe that a hostile external actor is likely to do less harm the less he or she knows or hears from the administrator. Lying low is a typical strategy in the face of hostility. Pursuit of internal strategies becomes the preferred course of action.

However, state agency heads do not completely withdraw from external relations in the face of misunderstanding, for the cost of such behavior might be too high. Departments facing misunderstanding may seek to educate or to prevent harmful action by external actors. Thus, the external task becomes one of prevention. For example, of those department heads (n=110) perceiving the legislature as one of the three least understanding actors, 46 percent characterized their lobbying as opposing legislation, compared to only 33 percent of the other (n=631) administrators ranking legislatures.

A factor closely related to the degree of understanding by the external actor in promoting an external orientation on the part of state agency heads is the administrators' perceived ability to control the external actor. In particular, agencies that claim to control local administrators place more importance on intergovernmental liaison. Of those administrators (n=83) reporting a great deal of control over local administrators, 43 percent chose such liaison as one of their three most important tasks, compared to 35 percent of those (n=324) administrators having "some" control and 26 percent of those (n=135) having "no" control. These data do not include those administrators reporting no local government administrators as relevant to their policy areas. Agencies are apparently encouraged to engage in liaison with external actors by friendly or controlled environments.

Consequences of Task Choice

The argument for control of administration by external actors (elected officials, in particular) is that of accountability. Administrators make public policy and yet most are not elected. Excessive separation of administration from politics may lead to an ungoverned bureaucracy with discretion to make important policy decisions. State agency heads included in this study reported a significant amount of discretion. In responding to a question about how much discretion their agencies possess in the spending of funds, 39 percent reported "a great deal," 46 percent noted "some," while only 15 percent said "relatively little" or "none."

Dependence upon external actors reduces somewhat the discretion of state agencies. For example, where administrators have as their primary task gubernatorial and legislative liaison, agencies have significantly less discretion in spending than do other agencies.[13] Thus, where administrators feel a greater need to be cognizant of elected officials, accountability (in the form of less discretion) seems stronger.

Similarly, state administrators focusing on internal tasks and thus having more separation from the control of external actors reported having more discretion than other administrators. While only 24 percent of those department heads (n=99) identifying the gubernatorial and legislative liaison as a primary task claimed to have a great deal of discretion in the spending of their department's funds, 39 percent of those (n=419) citing management as their primary task and 50 percent of those (n=171) citing program development as their primary task reported having a great deal of discretion. Independence or separation from liaison with elected officials appears to increase the policy-making powers of administrators.

In addition to its negative relationship with administrative discretion, another consequence of emphasis on the gubernatorial and legislative liaison task is its relationship to the different internal tasks. The ranking of the gubernatorial and legislative liaison task is more negatively related (gamma = -.49) to program development than to the management task (gamma = -.26). The negative correlations between such liaison and the internal tasks results in part from the fact that the importance of each task is determined by the ranking of the other tasks. Thus, a high ranking on one task lowers the ranking on other tasks. The key point here is that the relationship between the ranking on the gubernatorial and legislative liaison task is more negative with respect to program development than to management. In other words, control by the governor and the legislature apparently is less discouraging to a management orientation than to an emphasis on program development.

This finding raises an interesting dilemma, although certainly not a new one. Proponents of the separation of politics and administration argue that external control retards rational decision making and thereby inhibits effective program implementation. The finding reported above indicates that gubernatorial and legislative liaison and the influence of external actors implied therein does indeed discourage more than it encourages program development. Since program development suggests greater creativity in administration than does management, this finding particularly supports proponents of separation and is discouraging for supporters of political control.

Conclusion

Historically those in favor of curtailing political intervention in administration argued that it would eliminate corruption, inefficiencies thought to be connected with patronage, and preferential treatment associated with partisanship. The contemporary argument for limiting political intervention in administration is that policy decisions made by professionals are more likely to create efficiency and effectiveness in program delivery than are policy decisions made by amateurs operating in the political arena. Nevertheless, the democratic value of accountability requires that administration be subject to political control.

It is clear from the evidence presented in this chapter that the more agency heads perceive a need to engage in external relations with such political actors as the governor and the legislature, the less likely they are to be able to substitute professional policy preferences for those of elected leaders. Although political control of administration may inhibit the ability of administrators to manage, it is more likely to discourage program development. As suggested by the respondents' perception of various actors' understanding of their programs, control by the legislature is a greater threat to program development than is control by the governor.

An earlier version of this chapter appeared in *American Review of Public Administration*, Volume 16, No. 2/3 (Summer/Fall 1982).

Chapter 3

The Governor as Chief Administrator

In recent years most states have strengthened the formal powers of governors, especially budgetary and appointment powers, in an effort to increase gubernatorial control over agencies of the executive branch. However, it is not entirely clear how successful governors have been in using these powers to gain control over the administrative agencies of their states. Because of the short tenure of most governors and the difficulty they often encounter when attempting to penetrate bureaucratic routines, it is quite likely that the administrative machinery of many state governments remains under the control of administrators rather than the governor. In fact, some of the available evidence suggests that governors may not actively seek to influence state administrative activities. For example, Martha Weinberg's analysis of the Sargent administration in Massachusetts emphasized that the governor was more a reactor to administrative actions than a leader of state administration.[1]

As chief administrators, governors can be said to wear three hats.[2] They are formally in charge of management, program development, and external relations. The management role entails directing and coordinating the activities of executive branch agencies so that program objectives may be achieved in an efficient manner. The role of program development involves the formulation of new programs and the modification of existing ones. The

40

external relations role amounts to gubernatorial interaction with the legislature, interest groups, and policy makers at other levels of government. How the performance of these three roles affects gubernatorial influence over state administration is the question addressed by this chapter. Information regarding gubernatorial performance of these roles comes from a mail survey of administrative departments in fifty states. This survey is described in Chapter 1.

As defined in this chapter, gubernatorial influence consists of two dimensions. First, a governor's influence is evident if administrators take into account his or her policy positions when making their own decisions. Second, gubernatorial influence occurs whenever a governor has more impact on state agency decisions than other political actors. The literature on administrative politics indicates that a number of actors influence governmental agencies. Deil Wright found legislatures to be more influential than governors;[3] Marian Palley and George Hale noted the deleterious effects of federal agencies and grants (through "picket-fence federalism") on gubernatorial influence;[4] and the centrifugal effect of interest group and agency linkages on chief executive influence is widely discussed in the literature.[5] To be forceful chief administrators, governors must be able to exert more influence than their competitors.

The data reported in this chapter suggest that governors do not dominate the administrative branches of state government. When given a list of seven political actors and asked to rank them in terms of their relative influence on departmental programs and objectives, only 38 percent of state department heads chose the governor as the most influential (see Table 2.2). In fact, administrators tended to perceive the legislature as having more impact; 43 percent cited the legislature as having the most impact of all seven actors. Fifty-three percent of the department heads ranked the legislature as having more influence than the governor. All other actors were on average considerably less influential than the governor in their impact on agency programs and objectives.[6] Nevertheless, the combined influence of local and federal administrators, interest groups, and other actors, operates to reduce the impact of the governor on state agencies. Although the governors are the chief administrative officers of state goverments, they do not necessarily dominate state administration.

The governors are strong administratively (defined here as having half of the department heads in each state cite the governor as the political actor with the most influence over them) in only 16 of the states. On the other hand, as indicated in Table 3.1, the governor is very weak (defined here as having less than 25 percent of department heads cite the governor as most influential) in 14 states. Some will surely question these definitions. One may argue justifiably that being in charge of just half of the house does not make one its master. One may also argue that administrative departments are creations of legislatures and of constitutions and that greater legislative influence over state government departments does not mean the governor is weak. In any case, the conclusion from these data must be that governors do not dominate administrative branches of government, despite the attempts of reorganization efforts in recent years to strengthen their positions as chief administrators.[7]

Table 3.1. Agency Heads' Perception of Relative Influence of Governor on Administrative Departments by State

Proportion of State Agency Heads Ranking Governor as Most Influential		
Half or more	One-Quarter to One-Half	Less than One-Quarter
Maryland (91%)	Kansas (47%)	Oregon (24%)
New Jersey (82%)	Massachusetts (47%)	Arkansas (21%)
Kentucky (81%)	Wisconsin (47%)	Alabama (20%)
Rhode Island (73%)	Tennessee (43%)	Delaware (20%)
Hawaii (69%)	Nevada (42%)	Florida (20%)
New York (69%)	Washington (42%)	Mississippi (17%)
California (60%)	Georgia (40%)	South Dakota (17%)

*Proportion of State Agency Heads Ranking Governor
as Most Influential*

Half or more	One-Quarter to One-Half	Less than One-Quarter
Louisiana (58%)	North Carolina (40%)	Iowa (15%)
West Virginia (57%)	Minnesota (38%)	Texas (15%)
Alaska (55%)	Vermont (38%)	Arizona (14%)
Illinois (54%)	Nebraska (37%)	Virginia (12%)
Connecticut (53%)	Missouri (36%)	Montana (8%)
Oklahoma (53%)	New Hampshire (36%)	Colorado (0%)
Maine (50%)	Utah (36%)	South Carolina (0%)
New Mexico (50%)	Indiana (35%)	
Pennsylvania (50%)	North Dakota (33%)	
	Idaho (28%)	
	Ohio (28%)	
	Michigan (27%)	
	Wyoming (25%)	
Total 16	20	14

Note: Percentages were calculated by dividing the number of respondents from a state citing governor as most influential actor by the number of respondents from that state.

The Three Roles

The performance by governors of their three administrative roles affects their ability to influence the decisions of department heads. Before attempting to determine the effect of each gubernatorial role on the behavior of administrators, we must first define their occurrence. The literature suggests that governors are quite active in their role as public managers. Indeed, it can be argued that both legislatures and governors have taken this role seriously. The continued use of line-item budgeting and the continuing emphasis on efficiency in reorganization schemes suggest that control of operations rather than concern with program development is the overriding concern of governors and legislatures in their relationships with the administrative branch of state government.[8]

The governors' efforts to manage state agencies were measured in two ways. Department heads were asked if their governors had contacted them seeking improvements in operational efficiency during the year preceding the survey.[9] Department heads were also asked if their governors had contacted them during this period to encourage coordination among state agencies. Coordination among agencies has traditionally been regarded in the literature of public administration as a major part of the job of the chief administrator. The goal of improved coordination is often portrayed as leading to better program management. For some, the concept of public management implies more than concern for efficiency and coordination. Nevertheless, as used here the governor's public manager role consists only of this concern for coordination and efficiency.

Governors probably wear their second administrative hat (program activity) less frequently. The time, expertise, and resources of governors are limited; they must pick and choose their attempts to affect the administrative process. For the most part, they must be content with the hope that administrators will do what is right (not cause trouble and generate complaints). Governors are likely to find budget balancing to be more important than program content.[10] The governor's role in seeking to affect program activity was measured by the respondents' reporting any attempt by the governor in the year preceding the survey to affect the activity level of a departmental program.

The role of controller of external relations is not very often mentioned in the literature. At the national level, presidential efforts to control relations between agencies and Congress is a twentieth-century phenomenon.[11] At the state level, elected department heads, boards, and commissions limit the ability of governors to control external relations, even if they want to do so. Gubernatorial efforts to control external relations were measured by asking department heads if the governor had called upon them in the past year seeking to control their relations with the legislature and with federal agencies.

The data indicate that governors are more active as administrative managers than they are as program developers or as controllers of external relations. Sixty-five percent of the respondents reported contacts by the governor in regard to interdepartmental coordination and 53 percent reported contacts about efficiency. Only a third of the department heads reported contacts from the governor for the purpose of trying to affect program activity. The role of the governor as controller of external relations appears to be minimal. Only 10 percent of the respondents indicated gubernatorial contact aimed at controlling their lobbying of the legislature, and only 4 percent cited contact to control relationships with federal agencies. Although we do not have data concerning gubernatorial attempts to control relations with other external actors (e.g., interest groups and local administrators), we presume on the basis of data in hand that such gubernatorial efforts are also minimal.

Perhaps the lack of gubernatorial interest in program activity results from a lack of discretion on the part of administrators — i.e., administrators may be so confined by statutes which limit their discretion that governors need not concern themselves with agency activity. However, our respondents report that they enjoy a significant amount of discretion. Thirty-nine percent of the department heads reported a great deal of discretion with regard to spending funds, while only 14 percent reported relatively little or no discretion.[12]

As the lack of gubernatorial intervention regarding program activity is not explained by absence of departmental discretion, similarly the degree of interaction between agencies and external actors does not explain the lack of control of external relations by governors. For example, 44 percent of the respondents indicated they are "very active" in lobbying the legislature, and another 42 percent described their departmental lobbying activity as "active." Ninety percent of the respondents reported having contacted federal administrators in the year preceding the survey, and 84 percent reported contacting local administrators. One-third said they favored a great deal of interaction with interest groups. Clearly, department heads are active in their relationships with external actors. The lack of gubernatorial attention to controlling external relations cannot be explained by the absence of such relations.

Perhaps the lack of attention by governors to their administrative roles, especially program activity and external relations, can be explained by their acknowledgement of an inability to influence administrative behavior. However, our data suggest this conclusion is not warranted. For example, respondents were asked to identify those factors promoting coordination among departments. Fifty-seven percent cited mandates from the governor's office requiring coordination. Of those citing such mandates, 78 percent reported having been contacted by the governor in the year preceding in the survey with reference to coordination. The gamma correlation between citing such contacts and citing the governor as a factor in promoting coordination is +.57. As further illustration, 29 percent of the respondents indicated consulting the governor when considering requests from legislators on behalf of individual constituents. Such consideration was evidenced by 55 (70 percent) of the 79 department heads reporting attempts by the governor to control their lobbying with the legislature.

Decisions made with regard to coordination or response to such legislative casework may not have significant policy implications. Governors may often have little need to be represented in such matters. Administrators make other decisions which have far greater policy consequences. The significant amount of discretion held by administrators in the spending of departmental money was noted earlier. Surely, how administrators spend public money is of significant policy consequence. Do governors in the exercise of their administrative roles affect this area of discretion so pregnant with policy consequences?

Through their influence over the budget — particularly its preparation and execution — governors possess their greatest capability for influencing the discretion of administrators in the spending of money. While the budget is a consideration in all three of the administrative roles of the governor, it is most directly related to the efficiency aspect of the management role and to the program development role. The budget is clearly a significant instrument of influence. Two-thirds of the respondents identified the executive budgetary power as a significant factor in the governor's influence over them. This figure compares to 30 percent who cited the governor's appointive power and 36 percent who noted the governor's ability to influence the legislature as being significant factors of gubernatorial influence over them.[13]

Where the governors are vigorous in the use of their budget powers, the discretion of administrators in spending money is reduced. The gamma correlation between the respondents' perception of the budgetary power as a significant element in gubernatorial influence over their department and discretionary spending power is .16 (p <.05). In the twenty states where the average ranking of the governors' budgetary powers were greatest,[14] respondents in 14 of them reported less discretion than the mean discretion found in the fifty states.

Exercise of the three roles also affects the perceived relative influence of the governor vis-a-vis other external actors. Governors who seek to exercise influence over the programs and objectives of agencies apparently gain in influence compared to other political actors. As indicated in Table 3.2, correlations between the governor's exercising administrative roles (seeking coordination, efficiency, etc.) and the perceived relative impact of the governor on state agencies are all positive, though small. Governors who seek to influence administrative behavior are apparently able to do so. Yet the data strongly suggest that governors tend not to pursue vigorously their administrative roles, especially those relating to program development and control of external relations.

Table 3.2.   Gamma Correlation between State Agency Heads' Ranking of Governor's Relative Influence on Department and Governor's Performance of Administrative Roles

Governor's Role	Governor's Relative Influence	Statistical Significance
Public Manager		
Encourage interdepartmental coordination	.21	p < .01
Encourage efficiency	.21	p < .01
Program Level		
Affect program activity level	.18	p < .05
External Relations		
Control lobbying of legislature	.16	not significant
Affect relations with federal agencies	.14	not significant

The Limits of Administrative Roles

Governors seeking to be chief administrators can easily become discouraged, even if they pursue the three administrative roles vigorously. Governing boards and commissions and the use of the long ballot often encourage independence from gubernatorial leadership. Governors also face competition from other political actors who possess resources needed by executive branch departments. Finally, the administrative style of governors often limits their success.

Governors have traditionally suffered from the long ballot and the use of boards and commissions. While today governors appoint the majority of department heads, many significant ones remain outside the scope of their appointment and removal powers. This independence from the governor is said to encourage departments to look to political actors other than the governor for support and to pursue departmental goals contrary to positions of the governor. Independence also discourages a gubernatorial administrative role. Governors are most likely to pursue this role in their interactions with those department heads whom they have appointed. This tendency is most pronounced when seeking efficiency in management. Sixty-seven percent of those respondents (n = 495) appointed by the governor reported being contacted by the chief executive in regard to efficiency concerns; only 42 percent of the heads (n = 160) appointed by boards and 23 percent of the elected heads (n = 87) gave a similar report. Perhaps governors may be made to feel unwelcome when they seek to affect changes in the internal management of those departments outside their appointment jurisdictions. In any event, governors tend to limit the exercise of their administrative roles to those departments that come within the purview of their appointment powers.

Even if governors exercise their administrative roles, competitors may challenge their influence. Political actors external to state administration compete with governors for the attention and compliance of state administrators. Examination of those factors affecting coordination among departments and the administrative responses to legislator requests on behalf of constituents illustrate the significance of external actors on administrative decisions. As the reader may recall, 57 percent of the respondents indicated that the position of the governor was significant in promoting coordination. However, they also identified other factors.[15] Sixty-seven percent cited state laws mandating coordination and 64 percent noted the professionalism of state administrators as factors promoting coordination. In essence, the effects of legislative lawmaking are cited as often as the governor, and administrators cite their own professional standards as frequently as they cite the governor. The impact of the federal government on state agency coordination is not far behind, with 46 percent citing the requirements of federal agencies as encouraging coordination. Although governors tend to be very assertive in performing the coordination aspect of their public manager role, they are not unrivaled in this regard.

Similarly, in the matter of responding to legislator requests on behalf of constituents, the governor's position (cited by 29 percent of the respondents) was not the most significant factor affecting the responses of department heads.[16] Ninety-five percent of the administrators cited legitimacy of the request as a reason for their response. The second most frequently cited factor was the importance attached to the request by the legislator. Although legislators forward numerous requests to administrative departments, they apparently do not always care very much about receiving a favorable response. Thus, administrators possess a great deal of independence from the legislature and the governor in choosing their responses. However, legislative and gubernatorial positions are not totally neglected. For example, 22 percent of the respondents noted that the ability of the legislator to influence their program affected their responses. Thus, governors not only fail to get administrators to consult their position consistently, but they are also unable to protect executive departments from the interventions of other significant external actors.

The threat to gubernatorial administrative authority from external actors is even more significant than indicated by the above illustrations. The threat extends beyond coordination and response to legislative requests on behalf of constituents. As noted earlier, a majority of the respondents cited political actors other than the governor as having more impact on their programs and objectives. The threat is exemplified by the data in Table 3.3. As indicated in the table, as the perceived understanding of a department and its problems by external actors increases, the influence of the governor declines. These data suggest that as the closeness between a department

Table 3.3. Correlation between State Agency Heads' Ranking of Governor's Relative Influence on Department and External Political Actors' Relative Understanding of Policy Area Problems (Gamma correlation)

	Political Actors' Relative Understanding					
	Legislature	Federal administrators	Local administrators	Interest groups	Congress and President	Locally elected officials
Governor's Relative Influence						
Relative to all other political actors	−.14	−.20	−.13	−.17	−.13*	.00*
Relative to particular other political actor	−.15	−.58	−.71	−.63	−.66	−.53

Note: Relative understanding was determined by having respondents rank the political actors according to their understanding of problems in policy area.

* All correlations are statistically significant except for these two.

and an external actor increases, the relative influence of the governor decreases. This closeness may result from common understandings or from the ability of the external actor to affect the department.

Consider local administrators, for example. The stereotype of state–local relations, especially in a legal sense, is that of master and servant. However, studies of intergovernmental relations have debunked that myth.[17] State administrators often are dependent upon local administrators for assistance in achieving departmental goals.[18] In particular, state officials depend upon local administrators, to successfully implement state programs. Because of this dependence, 32 percent of the department heads reported calling on local administrators in the year preceding the survey to evaluate their program, and 54 percent said they had called on local administrators to obtain compliance with regulations. More significantly, department heads may turn to local administrators for assistance with legislators. Both state and local administrators often have a common interest in the programs of the state government department. The authority and funds provided by the legislature pay the salaries of both. One-third of the state government department heads reported calling on local administrators in the year prior to the survey for aid in getting legislative support for their department's program. Local administrators, being residents and voters in the districts of particular legislators, have a particular advantage in persuading those legislators.

State agencies have to bear costs for these relationships. Local administrators make demands in exchange for helping state officials. State government department heads indicated several ways in which local administrators seek to influence departmental policies. The most frequently used method of lobbying state agencies is direct contact; 70 percent of the department heads reported being called upon by local administrators in the year preceding the survey to explain local needs. However, more indirect and perhaps more persuasive means are used. Fifty percent of the respondents said local administrators had lobbied the legislature for policy changes in the past year, and 44 percent claimed to have been contacted by legislators on behalf of local administrators. Furthermore, almost a third (31 percent) noted that local administrators had stimulated interest group activity to influence departmental policy.

One result of this interaction is to reduce the relative influence of the governor. Of those department heads having significant interaction with local administrators,[19] 23 percent (n = 105) ranked local administrators ahead of the governor in influencing their department's objectives; only 6 percent (n = 671) of the other state administrators ranking the governor gave a similar ranking to the influence of local administrators.

Federal administrators and interest groups produce a similar effect. Of those department heads who reported calling for a variety of reasons on federal administrators, 27 percent (n = 330) ranked such federal administrators ahead of the governor in influence compared to 8 percent (n = 372) of those with more limited contacts. The impact of interest group interaction can also be demonstrated. Of those administrators who claimed that there ought to be a great deal of interaction between interest groups and their own agencies (n = 246), 11 percent cited interest groups as the most influential actors upon their departments (see Table 2.2). On the other hand, only one percent of the other administrators so ranked interest groups.

The external political actor most challenging to the influence of governors however, is the legislature. As the reader will recall, state agency heads ranked the influence of the legislature as greater than that of the governor. Legislative control over departmental programs, organization, and budgets make the legislature a most significant actor for state government agencies. However, not all legislatures equally reduce the influence of the governor. Consider Kentucky, for example, where the legislature meets only biennially. In that state only 1 out of 17 department heads ranked the legislature as having more influ-

Table 3.4. State Administrators' Average Discretion in Expenditures by Use of Legislative Committees

	States' Administrator Discretion		
	Great Deal	Some	Little
Legislative Use of Committees			
Least	9	7	1
Medium	2	6	1
Much	2	12	10

Notes: State rankings on administrator's discretion in spending was determined by averaging responses of department heads from each state. Legislative use of committees was determined by respondents' lobbying in legislative committees; state rankings determined by averaging responses from each state.

Because of cells with small *n*s, a chi square score is not shown, although the data are strongly suggestive of a significant relationship.

ence. A measure of the institutionalized strength of state legislatures is the presence of a strong committee system. Accordingly, we have classified the states by the tendency of administrators to characterize lobbying of the legislature as involving testifying before committees.[20] Using this classification, the data in Table 3.4 show the relationship between this form of lobbying and the perceived discretionary spending power of departments. The institutionalized legislature represents a significant mechanism for controlling administrative discretion. When administrative discretion is circumscribed by legislative activity, the range of administrative discretion subject to gubernatorial influence is likewise restricted.

The governor as chief administrative officer must not only contend with professional administrators' natural desire for independence, but he or she must also compete with other political actors for the support of state government departments. The story of President Truman's observation about General Eisenhower assuming the presidency after being a military commander seems appropriate here.[21] Truman mused that Ike would give orders but find that nothing happened because those who were nominally subordinate had loyalties and bases of support that enabled them to resist the chief executive's controlling and directing their activities. Governors surely must have the same experience from time to time. Even more interesting, perhaps, they often fail to give orders at all, or, as we shall see, give them in a manner not likely to produce results.

While external political actors are a threat to the influence of governors as chief administrators, governors are even themselves a threat to their own influence. It has already been noted that governors tend not to be vigorous in their pursuit of administrative roles. The weakness of governors stems not only from the diminished degree to which they pursue their administrative roles, but also from the manner and style of that pursuit. In short, governors do not appear to reward agencies for compliance with their position.

According to our respondents, governors tend to reward departments on the basis of rational and objective criteria rather than for such political criteria as support of the governor's position.[22] Seventy-one percent of the respondents indicated that governors base their support on the department's achievements, and 68 percent cited support based on objective needs within the policy area. On the other hand, 48 percent cited the governor's political philosophy, 21 percent the governor's campaign commitments, and 17 percent the governor's control over the department. In a sense, this difference suggests the triumph of professionalism over control by the chief executive — with rational, objective criteria being more important than political criteria.

Governors who reward departments on the basis of political criteria are more likely to influence departmental decisions than if they rely on objective, rational criteria. As can be seen in Table 3.5, administrators who are rewarded on the basis of political criteria are more likely to be responsive to the governor. Note that department heads who are rewarded on the basis of objective criteria are more responsive than administrators who fail to score high on either standard. Governors who fail to provide cues of any kind are not likely to be influential, and governors who use both are most likely to influence decisions.

The use of political criteria in rewarding departments increases the influence of those governors who pursue the various administrative roles. For example, of those department heads whose governor has called on them about coordination, 80 percent of those perceiving departmental rewards to be based strongly on political criteria (n = 143) cited the governor as a factor promoting coordination, compared to 63 percent of the respondents (n = 366) whose governor encouraged coordination but did not use political rewards. Of those department heads with governors seeking to control lobbying of the legislature, 69 percent (n = 26) of those whose governor used political rewards cited the governor as a factor in responding to legislator requests about constituent concerns, compared

Table 3.5. Percentage of State Agency Heads Responding to Governor's Influence by Governor's Criteria for Rewarding Department

	Reward Criteria			
Governor's Influence	*Neither Political Nor Objective (n=288)*	*Objective (n=312)*	*Political (n=82)*	*Political and Objective (n=96)*
Policy positions	16%	29%	45%	53%
Coordination among departments	43	60	71	79
Influential political actor	29	38	54	58

Note: If the distribution shown in each row was displayed as a contingency table with two rows, the chi square score would show a probability of less than one in a hundred.

to 43 percent (n=53) whose governor did not use these rewards. Thus, the style of rewarding departments affects the governor's ability to influence departments. Below, we shall indicate how the governor's style of responding to administrator requests also affects executive influence.

Administrator Use of Roles

Although governors are often not assertive in their administrative roles, especially those in program development and control of external relations, department heads often seek to use these gubernatorial roles to their own advantage. To determine the extent to which state agency heads sought to use the governor, we asked our respondents to reveal their reason for contacting their governor. The data in Table 3.6 provide a comparison between the activities of the department heads and the governor's. These indicate that the concerns of governors and department heads are often dissimilar.

While governors seek to be managers, department heads go less frequently to the governor about management concerns. Fifty-four percent of the administrators noted that their governors encouraged efficiency. Only 39 percent of the administrators reported contacting the governor during the year preceding the survey to justify their current program. Furthermore, only 38 percent of the department heads noted having called on the governor to seek assistance in interdepartmental coordination, while 65 percent had been called upon by the governor to encourage this. Although governors may want to be involved in agency management, department heads do not appear eager to have governors involved in their current operations.

Administrators were more favorably disposed to the involvement of governors in the other two administrative roles, even though governors were much less active in these areas. For example, 60 percent of the administrators went to the governor in the year prior to the survey seeking

Table 3.6. Percentages of State Agency Heads' Role Relations with Governor

Governor contact with Agency Head	Percentage Citing	Agency Head Contact with Governor	Percentage Citing
Public Manager		Public Manager	
Encouraging coordination	65%	Pursuing coordination	38%
Seeking efficiency	54	Justifying existing programs	39
Program Level		Program Level	
Influencing program activity level	33	Requesting program expansion	60
External Relations		External Relations	
Controlling lobbying of legislature	10	Seeking assistance with legislature	55
Affecting relations with federal agencies	4	Seeking assistance with federal agencies	39

approval of program expansion; only a third of the respondents reported that the governor sought to affect program activity levels. Similarly, department heads call on their governor in regard to external relations much more than the governor calls on them. As seen in Table 3.6, with respect to interactions with the legislature and federal officials, governors are sought more than they seek. Overall, these administrative roles of the governor appear to be more valuable to department heads than they are to governors.

Administrators apparently tend to perceive governors as willing to use their powers in favor of departments rather than against them. As noted above, governors tend to reward departments on the basis of rational, objective criteria more than on political criteria. Furthermore, agency heads who approach the governor are encouraged to do so because they perceive themselves as capable of persuading the governor. Twenty-seven percent of the respondents claimed their departments received support from the governor because of their ability to persuade him. In fact, those administrators ($n = 210$) perceiving themselves as capable of persuading the governor were more likely than others to call on the governor. For example, 72 percent of such administrators called on the governor for assistance with the legislature, compared to 48 percent of the other administrators. Seventy-nine percent of such respondents called on the governor in regard to program expansion, compared to 53 percent of the other administrators.

Except for the public manager role, department heads tend to use the governor more than vice versa. Governors are often newcomers to state government who respect the professionalism of administrators. They fail to use fully the significant political prestige and administrative powers (appointive and budgetary) that they possess. For example, our data indicate that those administrators going to the governor for assistance with the legislature tend to do so as a result of his or her influence with the legislature. Yet governors apparently fail to use their influence to control legislative–administrative relations.

Conclusion

It is apparent from the previous discussion that governors are not the chief administrators of state government — not because they lack formal powers over administration, but because they are apparently personally incapable or disinclined to use those powers which they do possess. Governors appear to be more inclined to seek to be managers rather than policy leaders.

One possible explanation for this phenomenon is that our societal definition of good government tends to be closely associated with such business-world values as efficiency, productivity, and balanced budgets, rather than with policy leadership. In this context, it is not particularly surprising that governors prefer low conflict and efficient management over the active use of administration to affect their own policy goals and objectives. A closely related explanation may be that the nature of the current electoral system requires that candidates for state-wide office be reasonably wealthy in their own right or that they have access to individual or corporate wealth. This feature of the electoral system may have the tendency to preselect gubernatorial candidates who perceive the task of governing as an enterprise in management rather than an exercise in policy leadership.

The implications for having governors who are managers rather than policy leaders are interesting to ponder. One conclusion might be that our states are now better run than they are governed.[23] Professionalism and administrative decision making based on rational criteria encourage good management within departments. However, the independence of each department does not lead to either good management or good governance within the state's executive branch as a whole. Such independence means that each policy sector defines the goals of state government from its own perspective. The absence of a chief administrator devoted to giving policy direction discourages goal aggregation and good governance. Failure to achieve such aggregation may actually

increase inefficiencies and lead to poor public management. Thus, the states may be neither well governed nor
well run.

An earlier version of this chapter appeared in *Public Administration Review*, Volume 43, No. 1 (January/February 1983).

Chapter *4*

The Limits of Legislative Influence

Because of the formal authority possessed by the state legislature, that institution has more influence over state administration than any other external political actor. In particular, the power of the purse and general lawmaking authority are two prerogatives which make the legislature the most influential external actor in state administration. However, the influence of the legislature is not unlimited. Many department heads have considerable independence from the legislature. Departments are likely to be less dependent on the legislature whenever they have sources of money and legal authority independent of the legislature — such as the federal government and the state constitution. In short, limits exist to the influence of state legislatures. These limits will be explored in this chapter.

The influence of legislatures on state administrators is also tempered by the resources and skills of administrators. Administrators have powerful allies within and outside the legislature. They also possess valuable information which legislators need to do their job. Use of these resources through administrative lobbying serves to limit legislative influence. While administrators lobby the legislature, they also get lobbied by members of the legislature. This lobbying is particularly threatening to principles of impartiality and neutrality in administration as legislators come seeking favors for constituents and districts. The nature of those requests, their impact on neutrality in administration, and how administrators reduce their impact illustrate further the limits of legislative influence. These limits are explored in this chapter through use of data derived from the survey of state administrators described in Chapter 1.

Institutional Limits

The principle of separation of powers divorces the execution of the laws from the making of the laws. Nevertheless, the system of checks and balances in American government allows each branch to affect the decisions of the other. Thus, through their lawmaking and appropriations powers state legislatures can hold administrators accountable. In the past, legislatures have also exerted influence through the process by which department heads were selected. Historically, state governments have utilized a weak executive structure that limited the appointive powers of the governor.[1] The selection of agency heads by popular election and by boards and commissions served to reduce the influence of governors over executive branch agencies and thereby enhanced the influence of legislative bodies. However, the demands of modern government have required coordination and centralization in administration not provided by the weak executive model. As a result, the executive branch in many states has since 1960 been reorganized to increase the appointive powers of the governor.

Almost two-thirds of the department heads included in this study were appointed by the governor. However, the heads of several significant departments are often independent of gubernatorial appointment. For example, in the fifty states, 45 of the attorneys general and 42 of the heads of departments of education are selected other than by gubernatorial appointment.[2] Where the governor does have appointive power, the influence of the chief executive is enhanced at the expense of the legislature. As illustrated in Table 4.1, the use of gubernatorial appoint-

Table 4.1. Percentage of State Agency Heads Ranking of Legislature's and Governor's Relative Influence by Method of Selecting Department Heads

	Appointment by Governor	*Appointment by Governor with Legislative Consent*	*Method of Selection* *Appointment by Board with Governor's Consent*	*Appointment by Board without Governor's Consent*	*Popular Election*
	(n = 314)	*(n = 180)*	*(n = 31)*	*(n = 125)*	*(n = 86)*
Relative Influence					
Governor's influence greater than legislature's	57%	55%	55%	25%	16%
Legislature most important external political actor	35	36	39	64	70

Note: Respondents ranked seven external actors (governor, legislature, interest groups, federal administrators, local officials, and Congress and President combined) as to their impact on the programs and objectives of agencies.

Percentages are calculated on basis of all respondents for each method of selection.

ment significantly reduces the perceived impact of the legislature and increases the influence of the governor. Thirty-five percent of the department heads appointed by the governor perceived the legislature as having the most impact on their departments, compared to 59 percent of those selected by boards and 70 percent of those popularly elected. The importance of the governor's power of appointment is even more clearly portrayed by the perceptions of department heads appointed by boards. Some of these officials must be appointed with the consent of the governor, although in most instances they are appointed without this consent. Of those appointed with gubernatorial consent (n = 31) only 36 percent cited the legislature as having the most impact out of a group of seven external political actors, while 64 percent of those appointed without gubernatorial consent saw the legislature as having the most impact.

These data indicate why legislatures have been so hesitant to strengthen the weak executive in state government. Abolishing boards and ending the use of popular elections to select department heads reduces the influence of the legislature in the administrative process. Even so, over a third (35 percent) of the department heads appointed by the governor identified the legislature as being the most significant external political actor.

The legislature also has other resources that help establish its superiority among external actors. A major legislative resource is control of appropriations. Without money, department heads will have no programs to administer. However, department heads are not helpless in financial matters. Some departments receive a significant portion of their funds from earmarked sources. State constitutions or statutes provide that revenue from particular tax measures must be appropriated for specified policy purposes. Among the most common beneficiaries of earmarked funds are state departments of transportation, which benefit from levies on gasoline sales. Perhaps as a result of these earmarked funds, only 27 percent of the heads of transportation-related departments classified the legislature as the most significant external actor as compared to 43 percent of all state agency heads.

Another significant source of revenue for state agencies is the federal government. Federal money must be spent for the purposes provided in the congressional authorization. State legislatures cannot reapportion this money to other policy areas. Twenty-seven percent of the department heads represented in our sample reported that their department received 50 percent or more of its funds from federal agencies. One-quarter of the departments received 25 percent or more of their funds in this manner. The effect of federal funds on the significance of the legislature for state agencies is clear. As indicated in Table 4.2, only 28 percent of the respondents obtaining more than half of their funds from the federal government saw the legislature as the most significant external actor, compared to 50 percent of those administrators receiving less than twenty percent of their funds from federal aid. Those program areas most clearly dominated by federal aid are those where state legislative influence is weakest. For example, only 12 percent of the adjutant generals in the state militia and 21 percent of the heads of state labor departments cited the legislature as having the most impact.

That federal funds result in administrators being less likely to cite the legislature as the most important external actor is perhaps not surprising.[3] However, the consequences of federal aid upon legislative impact is profound. Consider that 45 percent of the respondents from departments receiving half or more of their funds from federal resources ranked the legislature among the five least influential actors compared to nine percent of those department heads receiving less than 20 percent of their funds from federal sources. The appropriations power appears to be at the heart of legislative influence. When the power of the purse is significantly restricted, legislative influence is diminished.

Although aspects of the selection process for state government heads and the role of federal funding work

Table 4.2. State Agency Heads' Ranking of Legislature's Influence by Percentage of Departmental Budget from Federal Funds

	Budget Share from Federal Funds		
	Less than twenty percent (n=434)	*Twenty percent to one half (n=115)*	*One half or more (n=132)*
Legislature's Influence			
Most important	50%	43%	28%
Second most important	43	37	27
Third or lower	9	20	45
	102%	100%	100%

Note: Percentages do not always total 100% due to rounding.

against the influence of state legislative bodies, legislatures are still perceived by forty-three percent of state agency heads to be the most influential external actor. Administrators often seek to minimize or direct this influence. The major instrument used by administrators in this endeavor is lobbying.

Lobbying as a Limit on Legislative Influence

In response to a question about their lobbying activity, about two-thirds of the respondents indicated their department was active in lobbying the legislature. Twenty-four percent reported being very active in lobbying the legislature, and another forty percent reported being active. Only a third reported occasional contacts, and a mere three percent said that their department did not lobby the legislature at all. Clearly, most administrators play an active role in seeking to influence the legislative process.

Those who lobby the legislature do perceive their efforts as bearing significant fruit. Seventy-two percent (n = 165) of those respondents reporting their department as very active in lobbying cited this activity as one of the top four factors affecting legislative appropriations; only thirty percent of those administrators (n = 177) reporting occasional or no lobbying similarly characterized the effects of lobbying.[4] Administrators who lobby do so because they believe it pays. Lobbying is a way of influencing the legislature and thereby limiting the independent influence of the legislature.

However, active administrative lobbying is not a sign of legislative weakness. Indeed, the most lobbied legislatures tend to be among the more professionalized. As the ranking of the states according to degree of administrative lobbying indicates in Table 4.3, five of the ten states with the greatest degree of administrative lobbying were among the ten states with the most professionalized legislatures as cited by the Citizens Conference on State Legislatures. Only the unicameral legislature of Nebraska of the ten least lobbied legislatures was so ranked.[5] On another measure of professionalism (the provision of staff assistance for individual legislators), four of the most lobbied legislatures have such aid compared to only one of the ten least lobbied legislatures.[6] Thus, the evidence suggests that departments do not dominate legislatures through their lobbying, but in fact lobbying is often associated with legislative strength.

Lobbying is also at times a defensive strategy pursued by administrators. They may need to intervene in the legislative process to prevent what they consider a bad piece of legislation. The bill may be the product, for example, of interest groups or of a legislator. Over a third of the administrators (35 percent) reported lobbying more often against bad legislation than for legislation they had proposed or supported. This type of lobbying is done almost as often by those who have occasional contact with the legislature as by those who are very active.

Table 4.3. States Ranked by Average Degree of Department Heads' Lobbying of Legislature

1.0	Florida	26.5	Massachusetts
2.0	New Jersey	26.5	Utah
3.0	Minnesota	28.0	South Carolina
4.0	Hawaii	29.5	Louisiana
5.0	North Carolina	29.5	Montana
6.0	Missouri	31.0	Nevada
7.0	Rhode Island	32.0	Wisconsin
8.0	California	33.0	New York
9.0	Arkansas	34.0	Vermont
10.0	Illinois	35.0	Arizona
11.0	Idaho	36.0	Iowa
12.0	Colorado	37.0	Georgia
13.0	Ohio	38.0	Maine
14.0	Kansas	39.5	Oregon
15.0	Connecticut	39.5	Virginia
16.0	Maryland	41.0	New Mexico
17.5	Michigan	42.0	Nebraska
17.5	South Dakota	43.0	Alaska
19.0	Tennessee	44.0	Mississippi
20.0	North Dakota	45.0	Wyoming
21.0	New Hampshire	46.5	Alabama
22.0	Pennsylvania	46.5	West Virginia
23.0	Delaware	48.0	Texas
24.0	Washington	49.0	Indiana
25.0	Oklahoma	50.0	Kentucky

Note: Rankings are based on the mean score for each state of its respondents to question on degree of departmental lobbying activity.

Lobbying also tends to be more likely among respondents whose departments are particularly politicized. For example, department heads who are elected tend, with the exceptions of the secretaries of state and attorneys general, to be more apt to engage in legislative lobbying than appointed department heads. Of particular note are the heads of departments of education, who are very active in lobbying the legislature. The department heads of relatively new agencies also are quite active, especially heads of departments of consumer protection. Apparently, the creation of umbrella departments increases lobbying activity. By themselves departments of health and of welfare are not very active, but departments of human resources are quite active.[7]

The literature on lobbying suggests that it is a process of calling on those legislators favorable to the lobbyist's point of view.[8] Almost half of the administrators (49 percent) characterized their lobbying as calling on their friends in the legislature.[9] Among the administrators who were very active in lobbying, almost two-thirds (65 percent) characterized their lobbying in this way. Friendship is important, but influence also matters. Calling on those legislators with influence is a common lobbying strategy. Forty-two percent of the administrators perceived their lobbying to be characterized by such a strategy. Sixty-five percent of the most active lobbyists reported doing this.

Lobbying is more than just talking to influential friends. Most administrators probably do not have enough strong supporters in the legislature to win on important questions. They need especially to influence those legislators who are neutral. A major strategy is to provide neutral legislators with information. In seeking to do so, administrators face limitations. Although they may be viewed as policy experts, administrators may also be perceived as protecting their vested interests in trying to promote their departments. Another disadvantage faced by administrators in lobbying is their not being in a position to vote for most of the legislators they are seeking to influence nor to contribute to electoral campaigns. Even so, administrators are certainly in possession of significant allies.

The governor is perhaps the most obvious ally. Many of the department heads are appointed by their governor, who is therefore a potential supporter. The governor's position as head of the political party in power, the veto power, and the capability of determining much of the agenda of the legislature makes the governor particularly influential with the legislature. Thirty-eight percent of the administrators characterized their lobbying as to a significant degree involving calls on the governor for support. This type of activity was most common among those administrators appointed by the governor. However, governors have many friends and their interests are varied. Obtaining the support of a governor may be difficult. Furthermore, it is in fact the absence of the governor's support that is often an important reason for lobbying the legislature.

Interest groups are another important ally for administrators. Interest groups have some resources that administrators lack. First, interest group members have votes and money to contribute. Second, lobbyists for interest groups can be more informal in their lobbying. Lobbyists for interest groups spend much time socializing with legislators. This type of lobbying in itself is not particularly effective in gaining support,[10] but it does provide accessibility for lobbyists when they do need to communicate information. Administrators restrained by their professionalism and by their direct dependence on the legislature probably find social lobbying difficult. Administrators are likely to have little difficulty in approaching their friends in the legislature, but they may turn to the lobbyists for interest groups in seeking to influence neutral legislators and opponents. Access to these legislators is probably easier for the lobbyists of interest groups than for administrators.

Interest groups have significant reasons for working with administrators in lobbying the legislature. Interest groups want to enhance the budgets and programs of the agencies that provide services to their clients. Often the interest groups have been instrumental in creating the agency and its programs. Furthermore, the interest group's chances of being successful in the legislature are enhanced by the support of the state administration. The value of the information supplied by an interest group depends on its credibility, and the support of the policy experts of the state can greatly enhance its credibility.

However, the activity of interest groups is frequently stimulated by disagreement with administrators about priorities, so they are not always on the same side.

Many of the state administrators characterized their lobbying as seeking the support of interest groups. Forty-one percent of them characterized their lobbying in this way, and 61 percent of those most active in lobbying did so. As suggested above, administrators use interest groups for lobbying when they are perceived as favorably disposed to the departmental view. Of the administrators (n = 300) who characterized their lobbying as involving the use of interest groups, 20 percent ranked them as the most understanding external actor encountered by the department, in comparison to only 10 percent of the other administrators (n = 386).

Another potential ally for state agencies in lobbying the legislature are local administrators. Twenty-two percent of the respondents reported calling on local administrators for assistance in lobbying. Locals have a distinct advantage over state officials in dealing with the legislature; the former live, work, and vote in the districts of individual legislators. Furthermore, they are probably more capable of explaining to individual legislators the consequences of legislative actions for their districts. In essence, the local administrator is a more credible source of information for the legislator. Yet the local administrator is not necessarily an ally of state officials. First, the local administrator is often not dependent on state administrators for budget, appointment, or policy directions. These resources may be partially or totally under the influence of local administrators. Furthermore, the organizational and policy perspectives of the local administrator may be different from those of state officials. The local's perspective may be quite parochial and narrow compared to that of the state official. Interestingly, many of our respondents did not perceive themselves as exercising a great deal of control over locals. Only 93 of the respondents (13 percent) perceived themselves as exercising a great deal of control over local administrators; 46

percent said they had some control, while 20 percent reported they had no control (21 percent indicated they had no administrators in their policy areas).

Those department heads who tend most often to call on local administrators for assistance in dealing with the legislature are those who have the most control over them. Of those respondents who perceive themselves as exercising a great deal of control, 40 percent characterized their lobbying of the legislature as calling on local administrators, while only 12 percent of those with no control (n = 154) so characterized their lobbying. In seeking external actors to lobby the legislature, department heads look for those who can be trusted or controlled.

The strategies of calling on allies for assistance in lobbying are adopted most often by administrators who are least successful in their relations with the legislature. These strategies are apparently used when the department is having difficulty in its relationship with the legislature. Those department heads who gave the legislature's understanding of their policy areas compared to other external political actors a lower ranking than they gave the legislature's relative impact on their department[11] tended to use such strategies. In particular, these administrators tended to call on the governor, trusted legislators, interest groups, and local administrators more than did administrators not facing this dilemma. Seeking allies is a tactic frequently used in dealing with potentially hostile environments. Administrators appear to be no different from other lobbyists in this respect.

Legislator Lobbying and Its Influence

Lobbying is a two-way street. When legislators lobby administrators, they are often performing their constituent casework. Citizens, businessmen, and local officials probably have a feeling of helplessness in dealing with state administrators. For many individuals the processes of state administration may seem remote and byzantine.

The state legislator serves as an important link between constituents seeking access to and even influence over state administrators. For legislators the linkage role offers opportunities to prove they are good public servants and enables them to secure future electoral support. Constituents often do not know the policy positions taken by their representative in the state legislature, but they do know how these legislators respond to their particular problems with state agencies.

In their casework legislators may approach many different people in state administration — first-line administrators, heads of field offices, division heads, and heads of departments. The requests of legislators at all these levels may have significant consequences for the quality of administration, but the consequences are perhaps greatest when the requests are directed to departmental heads.

Legislative performance of casework may serve either to reinforce or to undermine basic administrative tenets. A bureaucratic structure is a purposive organization expected to make decisions according to previously established rules, to establish the rules according to objective criteria, to use the most effective means for reaching the desired goals, and to apply the established rule uniformly from one situation to the next. Constituent casework undermines these tenets when it promotes favoritism and partiality in rule application. Legislative casework reinforces these tenets when it performs the function of an ombudsman seeking to correct procedural inequities.

The bulk of calls from legislators tend to be those of an ombudsman type, (see Table 4.4). Favoritism is not the primary purpose. For example, the declining importance of patronage is clearly reflected by the data. Few calls are made to secure state contracts or jobs for constituents. Even with merit systems, state agency heads have some flexibility in filling jobs, and some calls of legislators seek to influence even that restricted discretion. The attempts to influence jobs tends to be most clearly pronounced in the southern states, especially South Carolina, Georgia,

Table 4.4. Calls by Legislators on State Agency Heads in Regard to Constituents

Purpose of Call	Agency Heads	
	Percent Receiving calls	*Median number of calls*
Information about departmental program	81%	10
Discussion of regulations	76	10
Complaint about service delivery	69	6
Project or service for district	66	6
Job for constituent	56	2
Contract for constituent	23	0.7

Note: Calls indicated in this table are not necessarily all calls to a department, only those coming to attention of department head.

and Louisiana. That 23 percent of the department heads were contacted about contracts and 56 percent about jobs in the year prior to the survey may sound alarmingly high and suggest that patronage continues to flourish. However, many of these calls may not have involved serious attempts to influence the decisions of administrators, but may have merely been to satisfy constituents who believe their legislators influence the decisions of administrators.

In seeking services and projects for their districts, legislators are certainly performing a function threatening to objectivity in administration. Two-thirds of the department heads reported calls by legislators in regard to such matters. However, even these calls may prove to be harmless. Consider the following case told to the authors by a legislator in describing his service to his district. He liked to snoop around the state administrative complex, not to check up on agencies, but to find out what they did. During his wanderings he would inform the administrators about his district and his needs. He was particularly likely to do his advertising at the Department of Industry and Trade; he would liked to take credit for new industries attracted to his district. This legislator has had a long tenure in his position.

The legislator's role as ombudsman is most clearly demonstrated by the frequent calls on department heads concerning regulations affecting constituents and complaints about service delivery. Jesse Unruh, former speaker of the California State Assembly, has noted, "Each legislator, depending largely on the type of constituency he represents, has a more or less heavy case-load of complaints against governmental agencies."[12] Constituents often have no other recourse against unfavorable regulations or poor service but to turn to their legislator. Only one state (Hawaii) has an official ombudsman to examine calls from citizens about state administrators. Significantly, the frequency of legislator intervention about complaints about regulations and service delivery is lower in Hawaii than most other states. However, the functions performed by an official ombudsman and a state legislator are not necessarily the same. The job of an ombudsman is to investigate complaints about arbitrary and inequitable procedures and to inform the agencies and the public of the existence of improper procedures. The legislator too can be an investigator and an advocate of proper procedure, but he can also be an advocate of favoritism in procedure. The job of the legislator is to represent the interests of his constituents; the ombudsman has a more neutral position in that he is an advocate for neutral and impartial administration.

The determinants of the administrator's reaction to the legislator's entreaties are crucial for explaining their effect on objectivity and neutrality. If an administrator's response to requests is based on possible consequences for success with the legislature, the administrator's decisions will favor those with influence in the legislature, and favoritism will be promoted. The legislature will thus be a significant factor in corrupting administration.

Administrators are not the pawns of legislators in responding to their entreaties, however. Most perceive their reaction as being based on the legitimacy of the requests. In many instances, administrators do not even have to make decisions about the merits of the case presented by legislators. Almost half of the respondents noted that their decisions depend on the importance attached to the request by legislators. That is, legislators make requests on behalf of constituents even when they do not perceive them to have legitimacy. In these cases legislators do not expect or want a favorable decision from administrators. Assessing the importance of the request to the legislator provides significant cues to the department head as to how much attention to give a request. However, the upshot of this process is that the legislator may become the decision maker and the guardian of neutrality.

The most damaging evidence of harm done to administrative neutrality by legislator intervention is presented by the importance placed on the individual legislator's influence by administrators in deciding how to respond to these requests. A fifth of the state agency heads reported making decisions on the requests of legislators on the basis of the ability of the legislature to affect their programs. One respondent wrote, "When the chairman of the appropriation committee calls, we jump." Fifteen percent of the respondents reported that the legislator's past loyalty to the department influenced their decisions. This suggests that some administrators see their response to these requests as ways to build support in the legislature. Rather than being at the mercy of the legislature, these administrators tend to lead the legislators. These responses also suggest that administrators may not be concerned about neutrality as much as they are about the survival and growth of their programs. Administrators are not always defenders of neutrality.

In general, the respondents tended to perceive more benefit than harm from the constituent casework of legislators. The questionnaire sent to the administrators contained a list of five potential problems or disadvantages resulting from such interventions. Interestingly, almost half of the department heads did not check any of the items. Many of the respondents either do not perceive such intervention to be a problem or they are not able to identify its effects. Perhaps of more significance is the 51 percent of the respondents who did perceive one or more problems resulting from this intervention. The greater the level of intervention in their departments the more likely were the administrators to perceive problems. Twenty-three percent of the respondents said such intervention distorted their agency's priorities, and 22 percent felt it harmed the morale of their agency. Fourteen percent noted that such intervention led to partiality in service delivery and 13 percent said it led to lack of strict adherence to agency regulations. These citations suggest that intervention does represent a problem for state administration. It can even hurt departments in the legislature. Thirteen percent of the respondents reported that such requests have hurt their support in the legislature. Apparently, there are perceived costs associated with rejecting the requests of legislators. Even so, administrators tend to perceive far more advantages than costs resulting from legislative intervention.

The questionnaire listed five advantages potentially resulting from legislator intervention. Ninety-two percent of the respondents cited at least one advantage. The most often cited advantage was that such intervention gives administrators an opportunity to communicate information to legislators. Given their perception of the low level of legislators' understanding of their department, it is not surprising that administrators welcome the opportunity to communicate information to legislators. Furthermore, administrators perceive such interventions as opportunities to gain information for their agencies. Forty-one percent said such interventions have improved the quality of service delivery and regulation as a result of legislators' information. Another 18 percent said that the information had resulted in their department's regulations corresponding more closely to the intent of the legislation. Overall, more administrators perceive such benefits than perceive administrative problems resulting from intervention.

The literature has often noted the importance of constituent services to legislators in winning reelection. As already noted, constituents may not know how their legislator votes, but they do know what help they have received with a governmental problem. Similarly, administrators perceive significant advantages in helping legislators. Forty-one percent of the department heads said that intervention by legislators resulted in increased support in the legislature. As noted above, only 13 percent said that such intervention had hurt their agency in the legislature. For most administrators, there is clearly a net benefit to helping legislators with their constituent services.

Conclusion

For many administrators the legislature is an enigma. One only has to attend a legislative hearing on a department's budget to understand the administrative dilemma. The questions from legislators often reflect the phone calls and letters of constituents. The head of a state's university system may be asked about why pay checks were slow in being delivered to workers at a small college in the system or why, considering the calls the legislators have received about lack of housing on the campus, a science building is requested by the system rather than a dormitory on a particular campus. Legislators approach higher education from a different perspective than administrators do. While increased professionalism in legislative bodies may serve in the future to reduce the inconsistencies in perspective, the values of administrators and of elected representatives are inherently in conflict. In coping with the legislature, department heads must adapt to a different terrain. They become partisans using groups and friends as advocates for their causes. Proponents of separation of politics and administration will argue that the result must be to destroy the neutral quality of administration. However, many of our respondents feel that such activities are necessary to encourage more informed legislative decisions.

The powers of legislatures are enormous, but not unlimited. Administrators must seek to ameliorate the harmful effects of legislative intervention while realizing that in a democracy professional values and preferences must defer to the policy choices of elected officials.

Chapter 5

Exchanges between Interest Groups and State Administrators

The importance of interest groups to administrators is well documented in the literature of American politics and public administration.[1] Interest groups have significant input in the formulation, adoption, and implementation of governmental programs. The nature of exchanges between them and administrators is often documented through case studies relating to national politics. These studies show that the relationship may constitute a subsystem involving the Congress, interest groups, and a federal agency.[2] But an extended examination of the relationship between interest groups and state agencies has not been undertaken. In particular, the literature does not contain a systematic analysis, involving a large number of agencies, of the types of exchanges taking place between administrators and interest groups. The literature suggests that in some states interest groups are particularly influential on state legislative politics.[3] Presumably they are also significant actors in the state administrative process. However, no evidence regarding the nature of that relationship has previously been reported.

In this chapter we describe the contents and consequences of exchanges between state government department heads and interest groups. The data to be analyzed are derived from our mail survey of department heads in the fifty states, described in Chapter 1. Although these data do not convey the outlook of interest groups, they do represent the views of the other side in the administrative–interest group exchange.

Theoretical Framework

In describing the nature of the interaction between state government department heads and interest groups, we rely on exchange theory.[4] Traditionally, in the relationship between interest groups and administrative agencies American political science has conceptualized the former as the more active partners,[5] as clientele representatives influencing the manner in which the more passive administrative agencies formulate policy recommendations and implement policy decisions. Interest groups have been "studied as independent variables in the policy process."[6] This approach underemphasizes the interactive and reciprocal nature of interest group–administrative agency relationships.

An exchange model of politics helps explain why interactions occur among administrative and interest group actors, and whose interests are served by the contact.[7] The central concept in this model is the relative need of each set of actors for the resources of the other. This determines what tactics will be used in gaining access, whether interaction will be recurring or intermittent, and which interests will dominate policy decisions, the administrators' or those of the interest groups. The character of administrator–interest group relations is, therefore, dependent upon the pattern of relative needs of each set of actors and the types of exchanges that result from it. Our data suggest four propositions about such exchanges:

Proposition 1: Exchanges are encouraged by mutual benefits. Mutually beneficial exchanges will be more common than asymmetrical ones in which one party needs the resources of the other more than the latter needs the resources of the former.

Proposition 2: In general, exchanges with interest groups are perceived by administrators as beneficial. Departments receive the greatest benefits from symmetrical exchanges involving mutual need and interdependence. In asymmetrical exchanges the passive actor who does not seek the resources of the other tends to be the loser. Such exchanges are hard to sustain. Most people expect to receive something in return for their assistance to others. In such interactions both parties tend to gain even though both make some sacrifices. In asymmetrical exchanges one party tends to sacrifice more than the other. Such exchanges may take place because one actor's persistence wears down the passive actor. The latter finds the experience annoying even if some small benefit is gained. However, our data reveal that factors other than persistence also encourage asymmetrical exchanges.

Proposition 3: Exchanges are most common when the resources of one actor are valued by the other. The relative values are affected by the actors' characteristics. The literature has often cited the significance of group attributes in determining group influence. For example, the size of a group may make its electoral support quite valuable to a legislator seeking reelection. Similarly, department heads look for certain attributes in groups. As group attributes affect the value of their resources, the characteristics of state agencies affect their need for interest group resources.

Proposition 4: Exchanges are encouraged by the institutional and cultural characteristics of the particular state. In general, state agencies need the assistance of interest groups to counterbalance the intervention of governor and legislature. States with political cultures emphasizing political participation tend to have a higher number of exchanges.

Findings

It follows from the first proposition that the state agencies calling upon interest groups for their resources will in turn be called upon by interest groups for departmental resources. Two cumulative indices for each department were computed: one measuring how many of the resources listed in Table 5.1 the department sought from interest groups, and the other measuring how many of the resources listed in Table 5.2 were sought by interest groups. These indices do not reflect frequency of requests for each of the resources. The decision not to ask about frequency was based partly on some skepticism regarding the accuracy of respondent recall, and in part on a desire to limit the time required to complete the survey instrument. Thus, we have used the number of resources sought in the previous year as the measure of need. As expected, the two indices (departmental need of interest group resources and vice versa) are positively correlated (r =

Table 5.1. Percentages of State Agency Heads Requesting Interest Group Resources

Resources	Administrators
Information about effect of departmental programs and regulations on interest group members	66%
Support for departmental legislative program	58
Information on interest-group policy position	57
Support for administrative regulations	38
Support for departmental budget	38
Support for department with local officials	16
Support for department with federal officials	14
Support for department with governor	14

Table 5.2. Percentages of State Agency Heads Reporting Requests for Departmental Resources by Interest Groups

Resources	Administrators
Obtain information about departmental programs	82%
Affect departmental regulations	76
Influence department's legislative program	62
Obtain new departmental programs	61
Register complaints about service delivery	59
Gain support for group's legislative program	49
Influence department's proposed budget	39
Seek department's support for group with federal agencies	30

+.63). Agencies seeking the resources of interest groups tend to encounter groups wanting their resources.

Using the scores on these two indices, we constructed a typology consisting of four exchange types. Two are symmetrical: the first indicates mutual dependence of each actor on the other for resources, and the second indicates mutual independence with little or no interaction. The other two types were asymmetrical, the "active" type among interest groups calling for resources from departments, where the latter were not interested, and the "active" departments, on the other hand, needing the resources of interest groups, where the latter were not active. Need was defined as requesting more resources than the median number sought by all departments or interest groups. (The typology of types and their frequency is indicated in Table 5.3)

Most administrators fall into the mutual dependence or mutual independence quadrants. That is, administrators either have a close relationship with interest groups or they tend to remain largely independent of groups. Only twenty-seven percent of the administrators fall into the

Table 5.3. Distribution of State Agency Heads by Exchange Patterns with Interest Groups

	Interest Group's Need for Departmental Resources	
	High	*Low*
Agency Head's Need for Interest Group Resources		
High	Quadrant I: Mutual Dependence 274 (35%)	Quadrant II: Administrator Active 91 (12%)
Low	Quadrant III: Interest Group Active 113 (15%)	Quadrant IV: Mutual Independence 300 (39%)

Notes: Interest group need is defined as the number of different resources sought by interest groups from a given department.

Departmental need for the resources of interest groups is defined as the number of different resources sought from such groups.

In dividing the variables into two categories we sought to use the median point. Because the data are discrete, and thus not easily divisible into two equal parts, the expected frequencies are not exactly the same for all cells. The expected frequency for quadrants I and II is 192 for each and for quadrants III and IV, 197 for each.

Percentages total more than 100% due to rounding.

asymmetrical quadrants. Exchanges are easiest and most frequent when there is mutual need.

The second proposition above asserts that departments receive the greatest benefits from symmetrical exchanges of mutual need or dependence. While exchanges and their patterns are interesting in themselves, of greater significance are their consequences — who gains and who loses. The stakes are quite high for the state government departments. Interest groups may help or harm departments in the agency's relations with the governor and even more significantly in their dealings with the legislature. The groups' demands and influence may distort priorities in programs and reduce neutrality of rule application. However, as indicated in Table 5.4, administrators perceive the effects of interest groups in a positive manner. For example, 50 percent of all administrators note that interest groups aid them in the passage of their legislative programs while only 14 percent say that such groups hinder it.

As seen in the table, administrators perceive interest group activity as tending to encourage more than threaten the impartiality of rule application. This is especially interesting, considering the commonly held view that interest group activity leads to particularism and special advantage in administrative decisions. The most significant objection to interest group involvement, cited by 21 percent of the respondents, was that it distorted priorities among policy areas. While departments and interest groups often work together, the influence of interest groups does cause a significant number of administrators to pursue policies different from those they would prefer to pursue.

Those administrators with mutually dependent symmetrical exchanges are the most positive in their assessment of interest group activity. Almost three-quarters of them perceived interest groups as being of assistance in the legislature, two-fifths said groups helped them with the governor, and over a quarter believed groups encourage impartiality of rule application. These administrators do not dictate to interest groups; the two are interdependent. As a result, they are not always helped by interest groups. For example, one-fifth reported that interest groups had harmed their legislative program. However, taking into consideration both the positive and negative effects, this set of administrators gain more overall than any of the others. Of course, administrators in the other symmetrical relationship (mutual independence) have few exchanges and receive the least from groups.

Table 5.4. Percentage of State Agency Heads in Each Exchange Pattern According to Effects of Interest Groups

	Exchange Pattern				
Interest Group Effect	*Mutual dependence (n=274)*	*Administrator active (n=91)*	*Interest group active (n=113)*	*Mutual independence (n=300)*	*All agency heads (n=778)*
Provide valuable information	79%	73%	66%	51%	65%
Distort departmental priorities	21	23	29	15	21
Aid in passage of legislative program	72	52	45	29	50
Harm passage of legislative program	20	8	23	7	14
Encourage support by governor	42	32	17	15	27
Discourage support by governor	7	2	7	3	5
Encourage impartiality of rule application	27	20	12	11	18
Discourage impartiality of rule application	13	4	20	10	12

The data regarding asymmetrical relationships suggest that the beneficiary is the political actor making the request. In those instances with active interest groups and inactive administrators, the latter suffer the most harm from interest group activity. They are more likely to perceive distortion in program priorities, more harm done to legislative program, and more damage to administrative impartiality than any other set of agency heads. They often appear to be faced with hostile interest groups. When the "passive" administrators were asked to characterize the behavior of interest groups toward their departments, 32 percent characterized them as unwilling to compromise, compared to a similar response by 16 percent of the other administrators. Apparently, these administrators will not, or cannot, prevent interest group intrusion in their departmental affairs.

The "active" administrators making more requests of groups than receiving them, reported getting favorable results. As indicated in Table 5.4, they tended to perceived less harm coming from interest group activity than most other sets of administrators, and they received much aid. Although they tend to receive fewer benefits from groups than the mutually dependent, they are perhaps in a more satisfactory relationship. Interestingly, the fewest number of administrators are in this classification.

In conclusion, these data support the first two propositions. Exchanges produce mutual support. When exchanges become skewed and a department receives more requests than it makes, the result is likely to be more negative for the department than if it were in a symmetrical relationship with interest groups.

The third proposition holds that one actor interacts with another when the resources of the latter are of value to the former. An actor's resource is of value only when he is capable of delivering it. What capabilities does a department head look for in interest groups in assessing the value of their resources?

The data in Table 5.5 indicate interest group attributes most valued by department heads. The most signifi-

Table 5.5. Percentage of State Agency Heads in Each Exchange Pattern According to Interest Group Attributes Facilitating Interaction

Interest Group Attribute	Exchange Type				
	Mutual dependence (n=274)	Administrator active (n=91)	Interest group active (n=113)	Mutual independence (n=300)	All administrators (n=778)
Influence with governor	33%	24%	23%	11%	22%
Influence with legislature	64	53	46	27	46
Previous support of department	68	58	33	32	48
Policy expertise	75	68	69	52	64
Representativeness of clients	60	31	33	21	37
Personal friendships of leaders with department heads	41	26	19	13	25
Common partisan affiliations of leaders and department heads	14	4	7	7	9
Organizational effectiveness	75	56	65	39	57

cant of these attributes is expertise. A close second is the group's organizational effectiveness, especially the activity and cohesiveness of its membership. These two factors indicate the need of department heads to reduce uncertainty in their program management. As noted above, agency heads reported calling on groups most often for information about the effects of departmental programs and regulations. The importance of such program management to administrators can be seen from the fact that when asked to rank tasks in terms of their importance for achieving departmental objectives, 55 percent of the department heads scored management as most important (see Table 2.1 in Chapter 2), ahead of liaison with the governor, the legislature, other administrators, and interest groups.

As seen in Table 5.5, department heads value groups' assistance with the legislature more than such assistance with the governor. As indicated in Table 2.2 in Chapter 2 they tend to see the legislature as having as much impact on their programs as the governor. More important, as suggested by Table 2.5 in Chapter 2, most (70 percent) of them regard the governor as more understanding than the legislature of their programs. Departments need assistance with the legislature. As indicated in Table 5.5, department heads look to groups that have helped them in the past for such assistance.

The data in Table 5.5 provide explanations for the behavior of the asymmetrical relationships. Fifty-eight percent of the "active" department heads noted that interest groups had been supportive of their agency. They request help from interest groups even if the latter do not often seek out administrators. This finding underlines again the positive nature of interest group interactions for these administrators.

The data in Table 5.5 also explain why "passive" administrators are open to "active" interest groups even if the administrators seldom request the latter's assistance. They perceive interest groups as having valuable expertise, which is clearly the most significant factor in Table

5.5 encouraging interaction between interest groups and all administrators. Another interest group attribute significant for "passive" administrators is the effectiveness of the group's organization. The louder and more cohesive the voice of interest groups the more likely it is to be heard.

It is well established in the literature is that some departments have a closer relationship to interest groups than do others.[8] Exchange theory suggests that such differences in department–group relations can be explained by variation in need for resources. The data in Table 5.6 suggest that the departments' characteristics influence the value of their resources to interest groups and their own need for such groups' resources.

Departments having narrow policy concerns are prone to exchanges of the mutual dependent type while departments having broad policy concerns tend to be involved in asymmetrical relations. For example, 7 of the 13 heads of departments of human resources (54 percent) in our sample are of the "active" interest group type, although only 15 percent of all administrators are of this type. In contrast, only 13 percent of the health department heads, 18 percent of the social service department heads and 7 percent of the mental health department heads, both functions that are frequently found as divisions within human services departments, fall into this asymmetrical category. This finding suggests the difficulty that the new "super departments" involving several policy areas may have in establishing harmonious relationships with interest groups of diverse positions. Also, 7 of 24 heads of public service commissions are of this type. These administrators are in the sensitive and difficult position of needing information from both utilities and consumer groups — a contradictory clientele. On the other hand, among those mutually dependent, the departments of mental health, agriculture, community affairs, and fish and game have narrow policy concerns and work closely with interest groups sharing common interests with them.

Table 5.6. Percentage of State Agency Types by Exchange Types

Agency Type*	Number	Exchange Type			
		Mutual dependence	Administrator active	Interest group active	Mutual independence
Mental health	13	79%	14%	7%	0%
Environmental protection	18	72	17	6	6
Natural resources	18	66	11	11	11
Agriculture	32	66	13	9	13
Community affairs	16	63	6	6	25
Fish and game	17	59	0	6	35
Health	24	58	0	13	29
Social service	21	50	9	18	23
Education	37	43	24	8	24
Insurance	19	42	11	26	21
Highways and transportation	34	40	14	14	32
Human resources	13	39	0	54	8
Labor	30	39	13	7	42
Commerce	14	36	21	14	29
Corrections	27	35	14	21	31
Higher education	20	30	10	15	45

Agency Type*	Number	Mutual dependence	Exchange Type Administrator active	Interest group active	Mutual independence
Banking	31	26	13	10	52
Public Safety	26	21	8	19	53
Public service commissions	24	21	4	29	46
Law	22	18	5	23	55
Administration	29	17	3	21	59
Revenue	32	16	19	22	44
Alcohol and beverage control	19	16	11	11	63
State	35	14	11	8	67
Economic and community development	26	7	29	14	50
Defense	15	0	20	7	73

Note: Percentages do not always total 100% because of rounding.

*Department types ordered according to descending percentage of mutual dependence types.

Interest groups appear to be more attracted to departments with significant discretionary authority. Compare banking departments with insurance departments. Both are regulatory in nature; however, banking departments are concerned with audits while many insurance agencies establish rate structures and thereby company profits. Perhaps, as a result, a quarter of the insurance agencies are in the active interest group category and another two-fifths are in the mutual dependence category, compared to ten percent and 26 percent, respectively, for banking agencies. Environmental protection agencies also have a significant effect on their interest groups, but the groups in turn have a significant impact on the ability of these agencies to accomplish their tasks. Thus, environmental protection agencies have the second highest number of departmental heads in the mutual dependent category.[9] The frequent inclusion of this agency in departments of natural resources helps explain the high percentage of heads from these departments also in the mutually dependent category.

Departments with politically strong clienteles are more interactive with interest groups than are departments with politically weak clients. For example, compare the higher level of interaction by heads of departments of public education with that by heads of higher education agencies. Also, note the relatively low level of interaction by correction agencies.

Departments with elected heads tend to be more interactive with interest groups than departments with appointed heads. For example, out of 37 heads of education departments responding to the survey, 13 were elected; of these, 11 were in the mutual dependence category. Of the 24 others (7 of whom were appointed by the governor and 17 by boards or commissions), only 5 belong to this type. Furthermore, appointment by the governor may discourage interaction in comparison to appointment by boards. None of the gubernatorial appointees was of the mutually dependent type, compared to 5 of the board appointees.

However, the data for heads of departments of agriculture do not support the above conclusion. Five of the 8 elected heads of this agency were of the mutually dependent type, compared to 4 of the 6 board-appointed heads and 11 of the 17 governor-appointed heads. Agricultural agency heads are quite interactive with interest groups regardless of the method of selection. Unlike the appointed heads of education departments, appointed heads of agriculture agencies were more likely to be influenced by interest groups; note the much higher percentages of education heads in the active administrator and mutual independence categories in Table 5.6. Comparison of appointed heads of education and of agriculture departments in regard to the attributes of interest groups that promote their interaction with state agencies produces some interesting explanations for differences in their behavior. On most of the factors investigated (see Table 5.5), the heads were quite similar, with two significant exceptions. First, 61 percent of the appointed heads of departments of agriculture (n = 23) cited personal friendships with group leaders as facilitating interaction, compared to only 29 percent of the appointed heads of departments of education (n = 24). Those appointed to be secretaries of agriculture tend to come from agriculture groups; the latter apparently influence the appointment process far more effectively than education groups do. Second, 22 of the 23 appointed heads of agriculture cited the expertise of interest groups compared to only 14 of the 24 appointed heads of education departments. Education officials have sought to insulate educational policy making from the political process; consequently they tend to be less receptive to the interest groups' expertise than do the state agriculture officials.

Data from most other departments do not allow a test of this hypothesis. Only eleven percent of all department heads had been elected to their positions, and the few departments with a substantial percentage of elected officials (departments of state and of law) did not have enough heads selected by other methods to justify comparisons.

The fourth proposition states that exchanges are encouraged by institutional and cultural characteristics of the individual states. Political cultures emphasizing political participation encourage a higher number of exchanges. In order to measure the contextual impact of institutional and cultural factors upon exchange patterns, we constructed an interval-level interaction index, which represents for each agency the sum of requests for resources both by the department and by interest groups of the department. Since it does not separate the asymmetrical phenomenon for special consideration, this index provides a more efficient mechanism for measuring institutional and cultural effects than would a nominal-level exchange index.

Interactive departments function in an environment of intervention by external institutions. Although interest group demand for departmental resources is one example of external intervention, departments use interest groups to cope with intervention by other external actors. For example, departments facing governors who intervene to affect agency policies and programs are far more likely to interact with interest groups. In order to measure gubernatorial intervention, we constructed an index based upon requests by the governor for departmental resources. This index correlates at +.42 with the interaction index. Similarly, we constructed an index of legislator intervention based on the number of requests by legislators for resources from each department; this index correlates at +.38 with the interaction index.

In essence, interactive agencies work in a more politicized environment than do agencies which are low in interaction. One measure of this politicization is the department heads' ranking of the factors affecting their appropriations from the state legislature. Correlations between the interaction index and the various ranked factors show a distinct need for interactive agencies to lobby the legislature. For example, the correlations between the interaction index and the importance of politically more neutral factors such as departmental achievements and objective needs within the policy area were −.04 and −.09, respectively. On the other hand, the interaction index correlates positively with the importance of lobbying the legislature (+.21), the concern of legislators for reelection (+.10), interest groups' activity (+.27) and the governor's position (+.11). As might be expected from these statistics, interactive departments are more likely to lobby the legislature.

The politicization referred to above is also illustrated by responses to a question asking about factors affecting the governor's support of the department. While the correlation between the importance of objective state needs and the interaction index with interest groups was positive at +.15, the correlation between the governor's political philosophy and the interaction index was +.32; correlation between the interest groups' support of the agency with the governor and the interaction index was +.38. Interactive departments must recognize these two external actors and consider the political needs of individual officeholders. These needs are communicated to the interactive departments by active governors and legislators.

The reader might suspect that the need of interactive agencies to lobby external political actors and the need to use interest groups to lobby those actors results from the department's lack of support by these external actors. However, that conclusion does not appear warranted. As already indicated in Chapter 2, we asked the respondents to place in rank order a list of seven external actors in terms of their impact on the department and their understanding of the department's problems (see Tables 2.2 and 2.5). Of those departments perceiving the legislature as having the greatest impact on them (n = 340), the interactive departments were not any more likely than less interactive departments to cite a particularly high or low level of the legislature's understanding of their problems. A similar relationship holds for the impact and understanding of the governor.

It follows that interactive departments coexist with strong external actors such as governors, legislatures, and interest groups. Their need for interest groups does not stem from any inherent weakness in dealing with external actors; it results from a political context that requires exchanges in order to accomplish departmental goals.

Interest group influence on the department is likely to be greater when there is no counterbalancing activity by the governor and the legislature. We asked the respondents to compare the impact of such groups on their departments with that of the legislature and the governor. As might be expected, the impact of interest groups is minor in comparison to that of these other political actors. Eighty-four percent indicated that interest groups had less influence than did the governor or the legislature. Exchanges with interest groups do not in themselves increase their relative perceived influence vis-a-vis that of the legislature or the governor. The correlation between the interaction index and the perceived influence of interest groups is .06 ($p < .07$). But it increases to .18 ($p < .002$) in cases with low levels of gubernatorial intervention and to .20 ($p < .02$) in cases with low levels of legislative intervention. Thus, high interaction between departments and groups does not in itself mean interest group domination of a department. If domination is to occur, it is more likely to happen where administrative oversight by the legislative body is weak or where the governor is not a vigorous chief administrative officer.

Although the value of group resources is affected by the activities of other actors, the political culture of the state may legitimize their interaction, thus reducing the cost of exchanges and increasing their frequency and value. Evidence of such effects on the frequency of exchange comes from response to a question asking each department head to select from among four options the appropriate relationship between the department and interest groups. The correlation between the interaction index and this measure of the legitimacy of interaction was +.33. Exchanges may not only be necessary but they are also perceived as being legitimate.

Table 5.7. States Ranked by Level of Interaction of Departments in State with Interest Groups

State Rank		Number of Departments	State Interaction Index (average deviation from mean)
1.0	Oregon	9	−.51
2.0	Colorado	9	−.50
3.5	California	13	−.43
3.5	Michigan	8	−.43
5.0	Maine	10	−.37
6.0	New Jersey	11	−.33
7.0	Minnesota	13	−.28
8.0	Massachusetts	12	−.25
9.0	Wisconsin	14	−.24
10.0	Ohio	9	−.21
11.5	New Hampshire	8	−.20
11.5	Florida	12	−.20
13.0	Alabama	10	−.19
14.5	New Mexico	11	−.17
14.5	Washington	12	−.17
16.5	Kentucky	14	−.11
16.5	Nebraska	14	−.11
18.0	Nevada	9	−.09
20.5	Arkansas	11	−.08
20.5	Delaware	8	−.08
20.5	Louisiana	10	−.08
20.5	Texas	8	−.08
23.5	Georgia	12	−.06
23.5	Arizona	14	−.06
25.0	Wyoming	10	−.02
26.0	Illinois	17	−.01

State Rank		Number of Departments	State Interaction Index (average deviation from mean)
27.5	Montana	8	.00
27.5	Utah	13	.00
29.5	Hawaii	10	.02
29.5	Pennsylvania	12	.02
31.0	Iowa	13	.07
32.5	Idaho	14	.07
32.5	New York	11	.07
34.0	Alaska	10	.08
35.5	Connecticut	12	.09
35.5	Mississippi	8	.09
37.0	South Carolina	9	.12
38.5	Missouri	14	.15
38.5	South Dakota	13	.15
40.5	North Dakota	12	.20
40.5	Tennessee	13	.20
42.0	Vermont	14	.24
43.0	Virginia	11	.27
44.0	Rhode Island	8	.30
45.0	West Virginia	11	.36
46.0	Maryland	8	.41
47.0	Indiana	13	.42
49.0	North Carolina	9	.49
49.0	Kansas	13	.49
49.0	Oklahoma	11	.49
	All States	558	

Notes: States ranked from highest level of interaction to least.

Only departments with responses from at least 13 states are included in this table. Deviations of each department from the mean score on an interval scale index for all departments of that type were calculated. The index scores are the averages of the deviations for all departments in the particular state.

The state rankings in Table 5.7 lend credence to the effects of political environment on the rate of interaction between administrators and interest groups. In the table, nine of the fifteen states with the highest level of interaction are classified by Ira Sharkansky[10] as having what Daniel Elazar[11] has described as "moralistic cultures." In comparison, only three out of the lowest fifteen can be so described. States with a moralistic culture have high levels of political participation. States with "traditionalistic cultures" are said to discourage political participation. Seven of the lowest fifteen states in interaction are classified by Sharkansky's interpretation of Elazar as being traditionalistic in comparison to only two of the fifteen most interactive states. Some of the states high in interaction also possess legislative bodies known for their concern with administration; for example, Colorado and Florida passed the first "sunset laws" in the country. New Jersey has a tradition of active government with a strong governor and a supreme court known for its judicial activism. California, Colorado, and Oregon are states associated with direct democracy and the referendum.

In summary, the value of exchanges is more significant in states where political participation is encouraged and where the institutional capacity of external political actors is more pronounced. Nevertheless, in political environments favorable to interest group–administration exchanges, groups are not likely to be able to dominate state government departments.

Conclusions

In general, interest groups and state agencies are allies. Groups are not seen by administrators as harmful; rather, they are viewed as providing state agencies with valuable resources. The benefits derived from interaction with interest groups are clearly more pronounced for some agencies than for others. Agencies engaged in mutual dependence with interest groups benefit the most from such exchanges. Agencies engaged in asymmetrical relationships with groups find the benefits from exchanges to be less frequent and less certain. In particular, agencies engaged in the active interest group type of relationship tend to have negative experiences with their exchanges. The mutually independent (39 percent of the respondents) had the fewest exchanges and allies.

Frequency and type of exchanges varied by department, by the interest groups involved, and by the institutional and cultural context. Such variation raises a number of significant questions about the effects of interest groups on administration in the states. Does it matter that groups and agencies have more interaction in one state than in another? Does it matter that departments prefer to interact with groups having policy expertise more than with groups possessing legislative influence? Does it matter that departments with narrow policy concerns have closer relationships with groups than departments with broader policy concerns? Does it matter that groups appear capable of reducing the influence of governors and legislatures over state administration? We believe the answer to each of these questions is yes.

Consider, for example, variation of interaction among the states. Our data suggest that administrative decision making is more elitist in states without significant agency–interest group interaction. Agencies go to groups seeking information and presumably they incorporate some of that information into their decision making. In states where agencies do not do this, they make decisions on the basis of their own limited information. Our data do not justify the fear that interaction with interest groups produces not only responsiveness to interest group needs but department subjection to interest group demands. But if interaction is not a manifestation of control by interest groups, could it be evidence of alliances between groups and agencies that undermine democratic control by elected officials? Is not the close relationship between interest groups and agencies with narrow policy concerns indicative of such alliances?

Alliances do exist. But evidence of the undermining of democratic control is lacking. Our respondents indicated that lobbying by interest groups had little influence over their appropriations from the legislature. Interest groups do not appear to be very important in subverting gubernatorial control over agencies. If there is a threat to democratic control of administration, we suspect that it results more from the lack of competence on the part of the governor and the legislature than from the interaction of groups and agencies. Given the tendency of these institutions to delegate so much discretion to administrators, it is perhaps comforting to see administrators consulting groups rather than making decisions like autocrats.[12]

An earlier version of this chapter appeared in *Polity*, Volume XV, No. 4 (Summer 1981)

Chapter 6

"Speaking Truth to Power" in the State Appropriations Process

Budgeting is at the heart of state government. There are probably no other recurring decisions more important to state agencies than the annual (or biennial) appropriations decisions by state legislatures. The budgetary allocation of state resources determines which agencies and programs will expand or contract and whose values and policy objectives ultimately will prevail. Although a substantial portion of the state budget is relatively uncontrollable in each fiscal period, competition among agencies for a share of the remaining resources is usually keen.

More than a decade ago Kenneth Howard published *Changing State Budgeting*.[1] The title of that volume was a double entendre — state budgeting was undergoing important changes, and further change, particularly greater reliance on rational decision making, would be desirable. The spread of rational budgeting techniques among the states since that time has been well documented,[2] but the role of rational values in state government decision making has been largely unexamined. This chapter explores the extent to which state budget officials perceive the two values most often associated with rational decision making — effectiveness and efficiency — to be important in the state appropriations process.

In the past, research on the state appropriations process has found pluralist politics and incrementalism to be more important in decision making than rational values. For example, the literature holds that agencies which seek to increase and expand their budgets are more likely to be rewarded in the appropriations process[3] than are agencies which practice good stewardship by emphasizing effectiveness and efficiency in the use of the state's resources. It is no doubt easier for administrators to measure their success in terms of budget expansion (current appropriation as a percentage of previous year's appropriation) than in terms of program effectiveness or efficiency. They may also prefer to gauge success against a standard over which they have greater control, such as administrative "process,"[4] rather than by a standard over which they typically have less control, such as program effectiveness. Elected officials are also thought to place a great deal of emphasis on such values as inputs, distribution of benefits, and the protection of sunk costs.[5] These are the values of pluralist politics and incrementalism, not rational decision making.

Despite the apparent triumph of incrementalism over rational values, throughout most of this century a strong case has been made for greater reliance on rational decision making in the public sector. While program budgeting and evaluation are commonly associated with this movement, efforts to professionalize legislative bodies and to strengthen the office of the chief executive are also part of the movement to enhance the quality of government through improved decision making. Although the case for rational decision making has not been confined to the budgetary process, the association between budgeting and rational decision making has been discussed extensively in the literature.[6] How have rational values affected the appropriations process in state government?

In light of the substantial literature documenting the lack of success of planning-programming-budgeting (PPB)[7] and zero-base budgeting (ZBB),[8] further examination of the use of rational decision criteria (effectiveness and efficiency) in state budgeting may not appear to be useful. However, the economic conditions and political climate of the past few years may be more hospitable to rational decision criteria than the circumstances of the 1960s and 1970s when PPBS and ZBB were introduced. It has been argued that rational decision criteria did not penetrate the budgetary process in those years because favorable economic conditions supported the distributive policies of pluralist politics and incremental decision making.[9] Under conditions of fiscal stress, where some state budgets are experiencing absolute decline and many are experiencing decreasing rates of growth, rational decision criteria may prove to be more useful in identifying targets for budget cutting.[10] Furthermore, the analytic capabilities of state governments have substantially increased. The increasing professionalization of state legislatures, the centralization of executive authority in the office of the governor, and the creation of state government evaluation units[11] enhance the prospects for a more informed incrementalism.

Evidence of the penetration of rational values in decision making is not totally lacking. For example, although Thomas Lauth did not find zero-base budgeting in Georgia to be truly zero based, he did find that the process improved the quantity and quality of information available to decision makers.[12] In any case, Michael Patton argues that rational values do get utilized in decision making, but not in the deterministic manner some proponents of evaluation prefer.[13]

For the most part, attempts to learn about what counts in the state appropriations process have been confined to studies of a single state. This chapter is based upon the perceptions of state budget officers and legislative budget staff; it explores the importance of rational decision values (effectiveness and efficiency) in the state appropriations process. As noted, the spread of rational budgeting techniques among the states has been well documented. The purpose of this chapter is to analyze the perceptions of state budget administrators about the relative importance of rational values in state budgeting. In short, to what extent are rational values used to "speak truth to power"[14] in the state appropriations process, and to what extent does state power use rational decision criteria in that process. Our data derive from chief state budget officers and legislative fiscal officers who responded to the survey described in Chapter 1. Responses were received from 48 of the executive and 45 of the legislative budget offices.[15] These responses represent the perceptions of participants in the process. Although perceptions are not always consistent with reality, we believe that they are often better sources of information than what are sometimes regarded as objective budgetary data. Anyone who has ever worked with state budgetary data knows that despite their appearance of objectivity, budget numbers are not easily compared from state to state because of the difficulty of knowing exactly what those numbers represent. Perceptual data obtained in response to a common survey instrument alleviates the state-to-state comparison problems which plague so-called objective budget data.

Agencies

The point has frequently been made in the literature that administrators have little concern for policy outcomes. Administrators prefer to be managers or to focus their attention on inputs, process, and outputs.[16] While perhaps less hostile to rational decision making than elected officials, administrators are said to have difficulty communicating with the policy analyst.[17] Is this lack of concern for outcomes visible in the state appropriations process?

The responses of state legislative and executive budget officials to a question about the fiscal attitudes of state agencies illustrate a relative lack of concern for rational values on the part of administrators. The respondents were asked the following question: "Which of the following best characterizes the fiscal attitudes of most state agencies?" From the four choices provided them, 46 percent of the legislative budget officials responding selected "seeking to increase services," 29 percent chose "seeking to achieve effectiveness," 15 percent affirmed "seeking to achieve efficiency," and 52 percent of the legislative respondents cited "continuation of traditional services" as most characteristic. The responses of the executive budgetary officials to this question were similar, but gave even less evidence of a rational viewpoint by administrators. Only 6 percent characterized agencies as seeking to achieve efficiency and 15 percent cited effectiveness as an agency attitude. Both legislative and executive branch respondents suggest by their answers that administrators tend to be either acquisitive (seeking to increase services) or are managers content to do today what they did yesterday (providing traditional services).

Administrators may adopt these viewpoints as the result of demands placed upon them by political actors. Perhaps, because administrators operate in a political environment, they tend in fact to be less supportive of rational values than they would prefer to be. Nevertheless, the literature[18] suggests and our respondents confirm that administrators have much discretion. Specifically, executive branch respondents were asked how much discretion they perceived agencies to have in the spending of their funds. From the choices provided, 58 percent of the executive budget officials reported that agencies have "a great deal of discretion," 40 percent said "some," while only 2 percent perceived "very little or none."

The freedom of administrators to influence the objectives of their agencies can be illustrated further. From a list that included agency heads, the governor, the legislature, the agency's clientele, and the federal government, respondents were asked to identify who determines the fiscal attitudes of state agencies. As might be expected, executive budget officials cited the governor and agency heads most often, 59 percent identifying the former and 81 percent the latter. Administrators thus appear to feel they have much independence. Furthermore, the literature has shown that governors tend to give agencies a great deal of latitude, especially in regard to lobbying the legislature.[19] Only 19 percent of executive budget officials indicated that governors seek to restrict what agencies say during testimony before legislative bodies on appropriations, and only 2 percent, just one of the executive respondents, reported that the governor threatened punishment for undermining the budget.[20] Again, agencies and agency heads tend to have much flexibility in their administration. Their lack of concern for rational values seems to be at least somewhat independent of external political forces. Their behavior as perceived by executive and legislative budget officers appears to result in part from internal values that they hold.

However, despite their discretion, administrators do exist in a political environment. The fiscal attitudes of agencies appear to be affected by the behavior of significant external actors. That is, where agencies emphasize effectiveness they are likely to be rewarded for doing so by the governor and the legislature. For example, in those states where more agencies are perceived by budget officers as pursuing effectiveness in their fiscal orientation, legislative budget officers were more likely to indicate that their legislatures seek information about agency effectiveness and executive budget officers to note that agency effectiveness is a factor in a governor's changing the budget office's recommendations. Furthermore, as noted above, 59 percent of the executive branch respondents did note that the fiscal attitudes of agencies was determined by the governor. Twenty-nine percent said such attitudes were determined by the legislature. Administrators are not independent political actors; there is no dichotomy between administration and politics in the state appropriations process.[21]

The fiscal behavior of agencies is affected by external actors because agencies are not the decision makers in the appropriations process. Agencies are dependent upon the budget recommendations of the governor and appropriations enactments of the legislature. Because these are the powerful political actors with the greatest potential to incorporate rational values into the appropriations process, we now turn to a consideration of the budgetary values of governors and legislatures.

Governors

In many states the governor's impact on the budget is directed through a central budget office. As a result, the values of budget officers may be as important as those of the governor. As might be expected, executive budget officers perceive themselves as having significant impact on gubernatorial decisions. On average, they indicated governors change less than five percent of their recommendations.

Professional budget officers might be expected to adhere to the tenets of rational decision making. The constitutional or statutory requirement of a balanced budget found in most states would seem to encourage them to emphasize effectiveness and efficiency in state budgeting. This is perhaps demonstrated by the 55 percent of the executive branch respondents who indicated that their state uses either program or performance budgeting, as opposed to traditional line-item budgeting.[22]

Has the growth of rational budgeting procedures which Howard described[23] in fact led to an emphasis on rational values in executive budget offices? Executive budget officials did identify effectiveness and efficiency as among the factors (see Table 6.1) weighing heavily in decisions on budget recommendations. In fact, 58 percent noted "past agency success in accomplishing its objectives" and 42 percent cited "an agency's reputation for efficiency" as such factors. However, the significance of these percentages is somewhat diminished by other data. For example, when executive budget officials were asked to identify from a list their most important function,[24] more than sixty percent of the respondents favored controlling agency expenditures ahead of assisting agencies to work

Table 6.1. Factors in State Executive Budget Office Recommendations for State Agencies

Factor	Percentage of Executive Budget Officers (n = 48)
1. Program needs	90%
2. Agency program's importance for governor's goals and priorities	90
3. Increase in revenues	83
4. Agency appropriations previous year	60
5. Agency success with objectives	58
6. Agency efficiency	42

Note: The executive respondents were asked the following question: "Which of the following weigh most heavily in your decisions about recommending agency budget requests to the governor?" The items or factors listed in this table were among eleven possible answers.

more efficiently and effectively. Central budget agencies may have adopted program budgeting, but they continue to operate for control.[25]

Despite the "rational" image of budget officials, central budget agencies are usually extensions of the political arena. Budget agencies are often within the governor's office, their agency head directly accountable to the governor. Thus it should not be surprising that 90 percent of the executive branch budget officers cited "the importance of the agency's programs for the governor's goals and priorities" as one of the factors weighing most heavily in their budget recommendations. In general, for budget officers, the governor's values are more important than rational values.

The data provide further evidence suggesting that rational criteria are not as important as they may seem (see Table 6.1). Ninety percent of the budget officers indicated that assessments of program needs in the area of the requesting state agency's responsibility weigh heavily in budget decisions. Thus, the lesson for state agencies seeking support from budget offices appears to be to demonstrate the needs of target groups or potential target groups rather than the effectiveness or efficiency of program delivery. Agencies seeking to expand their level of service are most likely to succeed when playing a "more is better" strategy. Also likely to succeed are agencies pursuing a "maintenance of traditional services" strategy. Eighty-three percent of the executive budget officers indicated that the "amount of increase in revenues from current tax sources" weigh heavily in their recommendations. An incremental strategy is certainly compatible with an agency attitude "do as we did yesterday". That 60 percent of the respondents reported that "the amount of an agency's appropriations last year" weighed heavily in their decisions about recommending agency budget requests to the governor is further indication of the prevalence of an incremental outlook on the part of many state executive branch budget offices.

These data emphasize the importance of the governor in the appropriations process. This is also confirmed by the views of legislative budget officials — 43 percent rated the governor as having more impact on the appropriations process than the legislature. Thus, the significance of "rational data" for the executive budget office is necessarily affected by the values of the governor.

To determine the values of governors, we asked the executive budget office heads in what kinds of information (from a list that was provided) governors are most interested during their review of the budget. The responses indicate that concern for agency effectiveness is cited almost as often as "justifications for new or expanded agency activity" and about as frequently as compatibility with the governor's political philosophy or campaign pledges. However, only about half as many of the respondents cited information about efficiency as cited effectiveness.

We asked the heads of executive budget offices what leads governors to increase the budget office's recommendation for an agency.[26] From a list of five factors given to them from which to choose, the effectiveness of the agency was cited least often (21 percent). On the other hand, 77 percent of the respondents noted that increases result from agencies convincing the governor of their needs, and 65 percent said increases are tied to the governor's political philosophy. Thus, needs assessment and identification with the goals of the governor again emerge as the best strategies for gaining more resources — that is, in this case getting the governor to increase the recommendations of the budget office.

When governors use state agency effectiveness as a reason to make an increase in the budget office's recommendation, such decisions appear to be influenced by lobbying by interest groups and legislators. That is, agencies appear to demonstrate their effectiveness by persuasive testimony from clients and supporters. (See Table 6.2). Those respondents who say that governors change their budget recommendations on grounds of effectiveness are more likely to indicate that the governor is generally influenced by interest groups and legislators. Effectiveness appears to refer to client and supporter satisfaction. Such communication may reflect program success, but it is a biased source of information. From the perspective of the governors, the source of the message is probably more important than the message itself.

Overall, these data suggest that rational values are not very significant in the executive branch. Agencies tend to seek increases in services or to do as they have done before rather than pursue effectiveness and efficiency. In doing so, they appear to be doing that for which budget offices and governors offer rewards. These results suggest the significance of incrementalism and inputs in state government. "Power" as represented by the governors and their budget offices is not particularly interested in "truth" as represented by measures of effectiveness and efficiency.

Table 6.2. Relationship of Effectiveness as Reason for Governor's Agency Budget Increase to Governor's Response to Interest Group Lobbying and Legislative Support

	Effectiveness	
Other Reasons	Yes (n=10)	No (n=36)
1. Interest group lobbying:		
YES (n = 16)	7	9
NO (n = 30)	3	27
2. Seeking to satisfy legislative supporters:		
YES (n = 13)	7	6
NO (n = 33)	3	30

Note: Executive budget officials were asked the following question: "When the governor increases your recommendation, he does so because: A. of interest group lobbying; B. of his political philosophy; C. an agency head has convinced him of the agency's need; D. an agency head has convinced him of the agency's effectiveness; E. he seeks to satisfy legislative supporters." The cross-tabulation between effectiveness and political philosophy and need suggest no relationship.

Legislatures

Legislatures represent power in the appropriations process. Their power has been threatened by the establishment of executive budget offices under the control of the governor. Yet in recent years, with the establishment of legislative budget offices, legislatures have recovered some of their power. Thirty-two percent of the legislative budget officers reported preparing comprehensive budget documents independent of the documents submitted by the executive.

Even so, legislative budget offices probably have less impact on legislative decisions than executive budget offices do on gubernatorial decisions. At a minimum, the influence of the legislative budget office is tempered by the influence of the executive budget. Yet 49 percent of the legislative budget officers ranked their office's influence on the actions of the appropriations committees as greater than that of the governor. Thus, legislative budget officers perceive themselves to be an important if not predominant source of power.

The values of legislative budget officers are not dissimilar from those of the governor and executive budget officers. To learn what counts for legislative budget officers, we asked them what kinds of information they seek from state agencies. Again information about their need for money was most often cited (83 percent of respondents). By comparison, 69 percent said they seek information about effectiveness and 60 percent seek information about efficiency. When agencies lobby the legislative budget office, 85 percent of the respondents indicated that agencies seek to justify their need for money, compared to 50 percent who said that agencies seek to justify their program effectiveness. These figures do suggest that effectiveness is of importance, but only secondarily so.

In the legislative arena, power might be suspected of being unresponsive to rational criteria. Concern about getting fiscal inputs to satisfy interest groups and for funding distribution to satisfy constituents have been historically of major importance to legislative bodies. However, in recent years the amateurism so characteristic of legislatures in the past has given way to better staffing, more information, and better legislator pay — in short, to a higher degree of legislator professionalism.

The current values of legislative bodies in the budget process are perhaps best reflected by the actions of appropriations committees, the locus of power in the legislative appropriations process. An illustration of this influence comes from responses to a question asking legislative budget officials to what degree legislative bodies change the recommendations of the appropriations committees. Forty-nine percent reported the legislature making practically no changes, and 44 percent reported only minor changes. Therefore, to understand what values the legislature brings to the appropriations process, we must understand the values of the appropriations committees.

To ascertain what counts in the deliberations of appropriations committees, we asked the state legislative budget officials to identify from a list of factors the two most likely to affect the actions of these committees toward agency requests. As seen in Table 6.3, the most frequently cited factor was "justifications by agencies for new and expanded activity." Thus again agency need appears to be the most important factor. However, effectiveness and efficiency of agency programs were frequently cited factors. Effectiveness was second behind need, and efficiency was fourth. An incremental factor (the percentage increase that this year's request represents over last year's appropriations) was the third most frequently cited as one of the two most important factors. Interestingly, the distributive measures, such as support from client groups and significance for legislative districts, were cited by fewer respondents. These data suggest that rational criteria are important to legislative deliberations and that legislative bodies are not as political as may have been previously supposed. However, there are reservations to consider.

First, the perceptions of the legislative budget officials suggest that the behavior of the legislature as a whole is somewhat more political and less rational than that of appropriations committees. In particular, 24 percent of the respondents cited the significance of an agency's programs for the districts of legislators as one of the two most important factors for the legislature as a whole in decision making, compared to only 7 percent who cited it as one of the two most important factors for the appropriations committee. As indicated in Table 6.3, eighteen of the respondents noted effectiveness to be one of the two most important factors for the appropriations committees compared to thirteen who cited it for the legislature as a whole. Eleven of the respondents indicated efficiency to be one of

Table .3. Information ... Most Interest to Legislatures and Appropriations Committees in Considering Agency Requests

Information	Importance					
	One of Two Most for Appropriations Committees (n=43)		One of Two Most for Legislature (n=43)		Most for Legislature (n=43)	
	N	%	N	%	N	%
1. Justifications for new and expanded activities	21	49	15	35	41	95
2. Effectiveness of agency's programs and activities	18	42	13	30	35	81
3. Percentage increase over last year's appropriations	14	33	18	42	34	79
4. Efficiency of agency	11	26	6	14	30	70
5. Agency's abiding by legislative intent	8	19	11	26	38	88
6. Agency revenue from sources other than state appropriations	3	7	4	9	31	72
7. Significance of agency's programs for legislators' districts	3	7	10	24	22	51
8. Agency's support by client groups	3	7	4	9	21	49
9. Agency's meeting needs of individual legislators	3	7	5	12	11	26

Note: Legislative budget officials were asked the following question: "Which of the following kinds of information is the legislature most interested in during its consideration of agency budget requests?" The respondents were given a list of items (including those listed above) from which to check their answers.

the two most important factors for the appropriations committees compared to six who cited it for the legislature as a whole. Again, legislatures tend to be more political and less rational in their consideration of appropriations. However, the reader is reminded that legislative bodies are perceived by our respondents as making only minor changes in the work of appropriations committees.

A second reservation about the influence of rational criteria in the legislative arena is that legislatures tend to use them in a negative more than in a positive manner. The legislative budget officials were asked to characterize legislative changes in the executive budget each year. From a list of possible changes, 38 percent noted that changes were based on satisfaction with agency performance while 65 percent reported changes based on dissatisfaction with agency performance. In general, evaluation of performance is used against agencies rather than in their favor. On the basis of the responses, this tendency to punish rather than reward is the same for those legislatures and appropriations committees where rational criteria are important in decisions as for others. However, legislatures concerned with efficiency (as reflected by respondents indicating efficiency to be one of the two most important factors affecting legislative decision making) tend to pursue reward and punishment with a greater fervor than other legislatures. Ten (91 percent) of the eleven respondents identifying their appropriations committees as being concerned with efficiency reported the legislature as engaging in punishment and 7 (64 percent) of the 11 said the legislature engages in reward. The negative flavor of legislative responses on performance suggests that the emphasis on efficiency may be oriented more toward reduction of cost and less toward achieving effectiveness for the least cost. That is, legislative response appears to be more reactive than proactive.

A third reservation about the significance of rational criteria is the absence of symmetry between concern for agency effectiveness and efficiency. Only 6 of 45 state legislative budget officials identified both effectiveness and efficiency as one of the two most important criteria in their appropriations committees' decisions, and only 2 respondents reported that these two values were among the two most important factors for the legislature as a whole.

For some states, support of rational criteria appears to be more a matter of necessity than commitment. The two states where the legislature as a whole values both efficiency and effectiveness in agency operations, as the two most important factors in allocating state funds, had experienced revenue declines in one of the two years prior to the survey. In fact, they were two of only four states to have had such a reduction. Similarly, some states appear to be attracted to efficiency by institutional factors. Two of six states where the legislatures value efficiency as one of the two most important criteria have constitutional restrictions prohibiting debt. In essence, fiscal restraint, whether from a declining economy or from constitutional limits, is associated with concern for efficiency and/or effectiveness.

Given these three reservations, the significance of rational criteria in legislative bodies does not seem strong. Yet the commitment of legislative bodies may be greater than previously thought. As we shall see, this commitment does appear to affect policy decisions.

Consequences

Although effectiveness and efficiency are often cited by the legislative budget officials as being important to decision makers, our data have suggested reservations about the influence of rational criteria in the appropriations process. Nevertheless rational criteria are apparently not overlooked, and in some states they are more important than others. In this section we examine how their importance in these states may affect decision making and policies.

A distinguishing feature of states where rational criteria are used is a tendency to avoid pork barrel legislation in decision making. For example, from the data in Table 6.3, consider the relationships between legislative interest in rational criteria and significance of an agency's program for the districts of legislators. Four (31 percent) of 13 respondents from states where effectiveness is one of the most important types of information for the legislature indicated district concerns to be significant, compared to 17 of 30 respondents (57 percent) from other states. Similarly, none of the 6 respondents from states with legislatures having efficiency as one of the two most important considerations in making decisions about appropriations identified interest in the effect of a program on individual legislative districts to be important, compared to a similar response by 22 of the other 37 legislative budget officials. Also, respondents perceiving rational criteria to be important for their legislatures tended less often to note district concerns to be important in regard to decisions about changing the executive budget (see Table 6.4).

In legislatures emphasizing effectiveness, interest groups are perceived by legislative budget officials to have less influence on decision making. When asked to rank four actors (governor, legislature, interest groups, and agencies) as to their impact on appropriations, 16 (89 percent) of 18 respondents who identified effectiveness as one of the two most important factors affecting the actions of the appropriations committee ranked interest groups as least important, compared to 17 (63 percent) of 27 respondents from states where effectiveness was not perceived to be so important. In part, this stems from these legislatures and their appropriations committees' independence from interest groups with regard to information. Respondents from states with legislatures and committees pursuing effectiveness also tended to rank interest groups as a less important source of information than did other respondents.

Table 6.4. Relationship of State Legislative Interest in Agency Efficiency and Effectiveness to Budget Changes for Constituent Benefit

*Important Information**	*Changes for Constituents*	
	YES (n=23)	*NO* (n=17)
1. Agency effectiveness		
Yes (n=32)	15	17
No (n= 8)	8	0
2. Agency efficiency		
Yes (n=27)	12	15
No (n=13)	11	2

* See Table 6.2.

Note: Legislative budget officials were asked the following question: "Which of the following tend to characterize legislative changes in the executive budget each year?"

Compared to other legislatures, those that value efficiency are more often at odds with the governor according
to our sources. In such states, the governor is perceived by
our legislative budget officer respondents to have less
impact on appropriations than the legislature. For example, only 2 (18 percent) of the 11 respondents from states
with appropriations committees holding efficiency as one
of the two most important factors affecting decisions
about appropriations ranked the governor ahead of the
legislature, interest groups, and agencies in their overall
impact on appropriation decisions. On the other hand, 17
(52 percent) of the 33 other respondents ranked the governor as having the most impact. In the states where efficiency is perceived to be most important, respondents
tend to be far more likely to rank the legislature as having
the greatest impact. The resistance of such legislatures to
gubernatorial influence may result in part from governors'
lack of emphasis on efficiency.

Our data suggest that governors tend to place less
emphasis on efficiency than do legislatures. Only 47 percent of the executive budget officers checked "the efficiency with which the agency carries out its activities" as one
of the information items governors are most interested in
during review of an agency's budget request. In response
to the same question in regard to legislatures, 70 percent
of the legislative budget officials checked this response.
Furthermore, governors have a greater tendency to
increase budgets. Forty-seven percent of executive budget
officials characterized their governor as tending to
increase the budget recommendations of the executive
budget office, while only 9 percent characterized the
governor as tending to decrease their recommendations.[27]
In contrast, 40 percent of the legislative budget officials
characterized changes made by legislatures in the executive budget as increases, compared to 29 percent who
characterized change as decreases. Both governors and
legislatures tend to add rather than decrease. Also,
legislatures are making changes after the governor has
made increases; thus, perhaps there is not as much

pressure on legislatures to make further increases. Even so, legislatures appear to take a more conservative approach to budgets than do governors. This is particularly true with legislatures that emphasize efficiency. These legislatures are far less likely to make increases in the executive budget than other legislatures. Of the 11 respondents from states with appropriations committees valuing efficiency as one of the two most important factors in budget decisions, only 2 characterized legislative action on the executive budget as leading to increases. Seventeen of the 30 other respondents so characterized their legislatures.

The legislatures emphasizing efficiency tend to become more independent of the governor and to develop their own sources of information compared to those emphasizing effectiveness. They also are more suspicious of the executive branch in general, tending to give agencies less discretion and to view them as always seeking to increase services. This outlook contrasts with that of legislatures emphasizing effectiveness, where agencies and governors receive more favorable treatment. In these states agencies are viewed more favorably as a source of information and are less likely to be perceived as seeking to increase services. Emphasis on effectiveness seems to lead to a cooperative working relationship with the executive branch, while emphasis on efficiency leads to a negative one.

Overall, the use of rational criteria does appear to make decision making somewhat more rational. Interestingly, legislatures appear to be the arena (despite our initial doubts) where rational criteria have had the most impact. Generally, governors and administrators do not pursue or get rewarded for rational values. Some legislatures have created in the appropriations committee an institution somewhat more capable of being responsive to rational criteria. Those legislatures emphasizing rational criteria have become more independent of external sources of information and from internal pressures for pork barrel legislation. The tendency of legislatures to be more supportive of rational values is certainly an unconventional finding. However, it is not unprecedented. In an examination of policy analysis in California, Arthur Bolton makes a rather convincing case as to why the executive branch has difficulty in pursuing rational values.[28] The most significant attempt at rational policy analysis in the national government in recent years has been the work of the Congressional Budget Office.

Conclusions

The appropriations process in the states is certainly not driven by rational values. Although some may argue that rational values should always dominate political values, many would not be discouraged by the dominance of political factors in appropriations. As Charles Lindblom and Aaron Wildavsky have argued,[29] rational decision making is not necessarily superior to pluralism and incrementalism in the distribution of public benefits. Yet, if incrementalism and pluralism are to serve well, they depend on information to aid in decision making. Our data do not indicate that such information, at least with regard to effectiveness and efficiency, is utilized to a large extent. The data do suggest that such considerations are not totally ignored. Yet, where rational criteria are used, they are often used in a negative fashion. As Clarence Stone has noted,[30] the application of rational criteria may have detrimental effects on administration and policy. As rational criteria are currently being applied in some states, they often appear to be having such effects in that they are used in a negative rather than proactive fashion.

In this chapter, administrators are seen as being much more concerned with agency survival and program expansion than with effectiveness and efficiency. Even though administrators may be influenced to think in these ways due to pressures from the political environment, their values are similar to those of elected officials — both are trying to survive in a system of power relations and alliances. Yet, there is a more benevolent way to perceive this behavior. Administrators do not represent the whole of state government. Their jobs are to meet the needs of their clients (students, patients, the poor, etc.). Determining allocations among competing needs is the governor's job as representative of the entire state and the legislature's as a composite of the competing interests in the state. While this view portrays the administrator as another lobbyist in state government, it is not as negative as one which suggests that protectionism, empire building, and survival are the driving forces for administrators.

Part *II*

The Politics of
City Administration

A Brief Introduction
to City Government

During the twentieth century city government in the United States has been influenced in a fundamental way by the municipal and executive reform movements. The municipal reform movement sought to rid city government of corruption and those aspects of partisan politics which were thought to be associated with corrupt practices. Specifically, the reformers tried to end control of city government by machines based in political parties. For reformers there was not a Republican or Democratic way to deliver municipal services; party government was not needed. A non-partisan approach to city government was to lead to efficiency in the day to day activities of city administration. For reformers, partisan elections and the use of district elections for city council led to city government oriented toward interest groups and/or district demands rather than citywide needs. The result was more (and more expensive) services than needed.

In addition to non-partisan and at-large elections, the reformers proposed other changes in the governmental institutions of cities. The administrative powers of elected chief executives in many large and some medium-size cities today are substantially greater than they were fifty years ago. The budget power and appointment and removal authority of many mayors have been enhanced. Although the executive reform movement worked to strengthen the administrative powers of elected mayors in some cities, it took a different approach in other cities. Distrust of the political role of mayors led in those instances to the installation of a city manager form of government. Under this arrangement, a professional administrator was hired by the city council to serve as chief administrative officer.

Although it is common to characterize U.S. cities as being either reformed (city manager, at-large and nonpartisan elections) or non-reformed (mayor, district and partisan elections), hybrids in which a mayor and city council are elected on nonpartisan ballots are not uncommon. These institutional reforms have significantly affected city policies and the relationship between city administrators and the elected officials of the city.

Perhaps it is at the municipal level more than anywhere else that we have witnessed efforts to separate administration from politics. Through a variety of institutional changes reformers attempted to mitigate the influence of party organizations, legislative district orientations and electoral politics by encouraging non-partisanship and professionalism in city government. As will be seen in the following chapters, the reform movement not only affected the relationships between elected officials and administrators, but it also had a decided impact on the policies of city governments.

Chapter 7

Reform and Rational Decision Making: The View of City Administrators

This chapter examines the findings of a survey of city police, fire, and public works chiefs to determine if the goals of the municipal reform movement are in fact reflected more in the attitudes and behavior of officials in cities that have reform institutions. Efforts at reform in municipal government have focused on making decision making more rational.[1] In particular, the municipal reform movement sought increased efficiency, effectiveness, and equity in urban administration.[2] For the reformers, a caretaker orientation[3] of maintaining traditional services or an emphasis on increased services to gain political support were governing styles to be discouraged. To attain their goal of rational decision making, reformers recommended a number of institutional changes designed to encourage a new direction in urban administration. Chief among these recommended changes have been the use of nonpartisan elections to rid cities of political parties, the establishment of a nonpolitical, professional chief executive (city manager), and the use of at-large elections to discourage pork barrel policies in city councils.

The consequences of reform institutions for urban government are still not entirely clear even though they have been adopted by a large number of cities. It is important to know if cities with reform institutions pursue efficiency, effectiveness, and equity in service delivery while discouraging increased service levels or a caretaker orientation in city services. In previous research on this subject, Robert Lineberry and Edmund Fowler found that reformed cities tend to spend less and tax less.[4] However, more recently, using an interrupted-time-series model to measure the effects of changes resulting from reform institutions in eleven cities, David Morgan and John Pelissero reported that "in the long run, government structure may matter very little — at least when it comes to city taxing and spending policies."[5] While today's cities may be more efficient than in the era of machine politics, from the perspectives of Morgan and Pelissero the adoption of reform structures has had no effect on city expenditures and taxes.

Confusion thus exists as to the impact of these structures. The lack of clarity is compounded by the problems inherent in the use of revenue and expenditure data in measuring the goals of cities. Although such data are popular in political research due to their availability, they are frequently quite unreliable. Some expenditure items may be omitted from budget figures. For example, money from other levels of government may not be included, and the use of special purpose governments for service delivery may hide substantial expenditure amounts.

The lack of clarity about the impact of municipal reform is further exacerbated by the fact that low expenditures do not in themselves mean that city officials are pursuing efficiency; nor does the absence of change in expenditure patterns following changes in a city's government structure mean that officials do not change their attitudes toward efficiency and effectiveness. That two cities spend the same amount of money for law enforcement does not indicate much about the quality of police work or the status of law and order in those cities. Similarly, revenue and expenditure figures are not always helpful in determining if city officials have sought to increase or decrease the level of municipal services. In short, aggregate data can often be misleading when attempting to explain individual attitudes and behavior.[6] In order to determine if administrators in reform cities and nonreform cities differ in their service delivery goals, we conducted a survey of those individuals with direct responsibility for providing three traditional municipal services. This survey is described in Chapter 1.

Definition of Reform

Department heads were classified according to a scale of municipal reform that was based on city government characteristics. The "most reformed" cities were those having a city manager form of government, at-large elections for city council, and low levels of party activity, while the "most nonreformed" cities had none of these traits. Cities with at least two of these characteristics are considered to be "reformed" cities. Form of government was determined by information obtained from the *Municipal Year Book*. The method of election (at-large, district, or a mixture of at-large and district) and the level of party activity in a city were ascertained by questions asked of the respondents.[7]

As should be expected, cities having one of these municipal reform institutions are likely to have the other reform characteristics. In particular, Table 7.1 reveals that cities having a city manager form of government have a stronger tendency than mayoral cities to have at-large elections and low levels of party activity. For example, of those city department heads reporting their cities as having at-large elections, 47 percent reported active or very active political parties, compared to 65 percent of the department heads from those cities with district elections and 63 percent in those cities having a mixture of at-large and district elections.

Even though municipal reforms are interrelated, the reform institutions may not have an additive effect.[8] That is, one reform component may have a greater effect on a dependent variable than the others. For example, the presence of a city manager in a city would obviously be more important in establishing a linkage between the presence of reform and a chief executive's emphasis on efficiency than would the presence of one or both of the other two reform institutions. For the most part, our purpose is not to establish the linkage of each municipal reform component to each dependent variable (attitudes or behavior of city officials). Often, as in the case already mentioned of city managers and the attitudes of their chief executives toward efficiency, the linkages are predictable. But by using an additive model for the municipal reform scale, we lessen the likelihood of establishing clear linear relationships and reduce our chances of establishing linkages between particular reforms and specific behaviors. In any case, discussion of interaction effects would lead to speculation and hypothesis testing that we wish to defer for another time. However, our data so consistently point to linkages that we believe our conclusions about reform and behavior are strongly supported without having to examine the effects of each component. Furthermore, since the attitudes and behavior of municipal administrators constitute a significant part of our analysis and since none of the three municipal reforms is specifically oriented toward these officials, determination of the specific effects of each reform institution or of their combinations did not seem as important as discovering the impact of an overall environment of reform.

To learn about the behavior of officials in reformed and nonreformed cities, the respondents were asked to identify their own goals and behavior as well as that of the chief executive officer and the city council. Again, officials in reformed cities would be expected to stress efficiency, effectiveness, and equity in service delivery more than would officials from nonreformed cities; the latter would be expected to stress increase in services and maintenance of traditional services. We now turn to an examin-

Table 7.1. City Manager and Mayoral Cities According to At-large Elections and Political Party Activity Level

	Form of Government*	
	City Manager (n=312)	Mayoral (n=191)
*Council Elections***		
At large	62%	37%
Both at-large and district	18	30
District	21	33
	101%	100%
*City Party Activity***		
Little or no activity	59%	23%
Active	27	36
Very active	14	41
	100%	100%

Note: Some percentages do not total 100% due to rounding.

 * Based on *Municipal Year Book, 1977.*

** Based on city department heads' reports.

ation of the behavior of city officials as perceived by city administrators.

Findings

Municipal department heads were asked to rank five objectives (efficiency, effectiveness, increased services, maintenance of traditional services, and equity in service delivery) in terms of importance for their department. Effectiveness and efficiency are the most highly ranked of the five objectives. Forty-two percent of the respondents ranked effectiveness in services as their first objective, and 32 percent ranked efficiency as their first objective. The other objectives were of less importance; only 9 percent cited maintaining traditional services, 8 percent increasing services, and 3 percent equity as their first choice.

As indicated by the data in Table 7.2, respondents from reformed cities tend to differ in the expected direction from respondents in nonreformed cities in ranking the objectives. Respondents from the "most reformed" cities ranked effectiveness, efficiency, and equity higher, and increasing services and maintaining traditional services lower than respondents from the "most nonreformed" cities. These data do not indicate that the relationship between municipal reform and the ranking of the objectives is linear. That is, administrators in merely "reformed" cities do not appear to differ from administrators of "nonreformed" or even "most nonreformed" cities in regard to the percentages choosing efficiency, effectiveness, and maintenance of traditional services. The difference between administrators is greatest for those in the "most reformed" and those in the "most nonreformed" cities or categories.

As administrators from the "most reformed" cities tend to differ in their views from those in the "most nonreformed" cities, they differ also in their backgrounds. Twenty-seven percent of the 120 respondents from the "most reformed" cities were affiliated with a municipal department in another city prior to assuming their current positions, compared to 10 percent of those respondents (n = 157) from the "most nonreformed" cities. Apparently cities with reform institutions are more likely to look elsewhere for administrative talent than are nonreformed cities. Furthermore, department heads in nonreformed cities are more likely to lack bachelor degrees. Thirty-seven percent of those respondents from the "most nonreformed" cities reported not having achieved this degree, compared to 22 percent of those from the "most reformed" cities. In short, department heads from "most reformed" cities tend to be more mobile, better educated, and probably somewhat more professional.[9]

That municipal reform is related to the backgrounds and objectives of administrators is an important factor in

Table 7.2. Percentages of City Department Heads' Rankings of Departmental Objectives' Importance by Degree of Municipal Reform

Degree of Municipal Reform**	Operational Efficiency First or Second	Service Effectiveness First	Importance* Service Delivery Equity First, Second, or Third	Maintaining Traditional Services First, Second, or Third	Increasing Service Levels First or Second
Most reformed (n=120)	76%	51%	32%	19%	16%
Reformed (n=94)	60%	44%	28%	26%	22%
Nonreformed (n=158)	62%	39%	23%	30%	27%
Most nonreformed (n=157)	61%	41%	21%	25%	29%

* Respondents ranked the objectives as to their importance for their department. Rankings are those with greatest difference between "most reformed" and "most nonreformed" cities.

** "Most reformed" cities are those with a council–manager government, at-large elections, and little or no political party activity.

establishing their linkage to city policy. The literature on urban administration makes it clear that city administrators participate in policy making through their exercise of discretion and their expertise.[10] Another administrator with significant policy making powers is the chief executive officer. Our respondents tended to identify the chief executive officer as having considerably more impact on departments than the city council. The municipal and executive reform movements paid considerable attention to the office of the chief executive. First, they attempted to neutralize it politically, and second they tried to make it the focus of professional management. Using the perceptions of city department heads, we were able to explore the relationship between the municipal reform index and the objectives of city managers.

According to our respondents, chief executives in the municipal reform cities emphasize the objectives of efficiency, effectiveness, and equity in service delivery. The data in Table 7.3 generally support the predicted differences between "reformed" and "nonreformed" cities more than data in Table 7.2 about the department heads' own objectives. Again, the data are more supportive of our expectations if attention is focused on differences between chief executives in the "most reformed" and "most nonreformed" cities.

That chief executives in "reformed" cities are more committed to the values of the municipal reform movement than their department heads is not surprising. The chief executives in the "most reformed" cities are city managers, many of whom have received formal education and professional socialization in the goals of the municipal reform movement. Furthermore, department heads perceive the city from the perspectives of their own department, a distinctly different perspective from the generalist view of the chief executive officer.

In any case, the differences in objectives apparently are carried over into the contrasts in the behavior of the chief executives in the two types of cities. City department heads were asked to indicate, from a list of items provided

Table 7.3.   Percentages of City Department Heads' Rankings of Departmental Objectives' Importance for City Chief Executive by Degree of Municipal Reform

Degree of Municipal Reform	Operational Efficiency First or Second	Service Effectiveness First or Second	Importance *		Increasing Service Levels First or Second
			Service Delivery Equity First, Second, or Third	Maintaining Traditional Services First, Second, or Third	
Most reformed (n=120)	79%	75%	33%	19%	21%
Reformed (n=94)	60%	76%	36%	29%	23%
Nonreformed (n=158)	61%	72%	20%	29%	33%
Most nonreformed (n=157)	59%	64%	22%	29%	38%

* Respondents ranked the objectives as to their importance for their chief executive. Rankings are those with greatest difference between "most reformed" and "most nonreformed" cities.

them, their department's operations most rewarded by their chief executive. Three of the items are particularly related to the objectives of the municipal reform movement: efficiency in operation, program accomplishment, and objective needs within the policy area. The differences are not large with respect to the efficiency measure: 82 percent of the administrators in the "most reformed" cities (n = 120) reported that their chief executive rewards them for efficiency, compared to only 76 percent of the department heads from the "most nonreformed" cities (n = 157).

The differences are more distinct with regard to the two other objectives. In regard to program accomplishment (effectiveness), 73 percent of the administrators in the "most reformed" cities cited being rewarded for program accomplishment, in comparison to 56 percent of the department heads from the "most nonreformed" cities. As for objective need, 45 percent of the administrators from the "most reformed" cities reported being rewarded on this basis compared to 32 percent of the respondents from the "most nonreformed" cities. Chief executives in municipal reform cities approach and execute their jobs differently than do their counterparts in nonreformed cities.

Although our study and the literature indicate that chief executives and their administrators are significant policy makers, it would be a mistake to overlook the city council. According to city charters, the council is responsible for making policy. Although the literature indicates that policy seldom originates with the council,[11] it must approve many policy matters, the most important of which is the budget. Another reason for examining the behavior of the council is that the municipal reform movement looked to the council as an important instrument for fulfilling its goals. The use of nonpartisan, at-large elections in selecting the city council was supposed to encourage a more rational approach to policy making in the city.[12]

On the basis of our survey data, it would appear that the reformers did achieve what they sought, councils that are less political and more rational in behavior. Respondents were asked to indicate those things for which their departments were rewarded by the city council. Several items are particularly appropriate to the question addressed by this chapter. Eighty percent of the respondents from the "most reformed" cities reported being rewarded by their city council for program accomplishments, compared to 64 percent of the respondents from the "most nonreformed" cities. Furthermore, 18 percent of the respondents from the latter cities reported being rewarded for providing services for the districts of particular council members; only 3 percent of the department heads in the "most reformed" cities reported such rewards. These differences can also be illustrated by the reported behavior of individual councilpersons; respondents from the "most reformed" cities were less likely (26 percent to 66 percent) than those respondents from the "most nonreformed" cities to indicate that councilpersons had called on them in the past year seeking projects or more services for their districts. However, the data are not uniform in their support of the argument that reform institutions make a difference in favor of more rational, less political, policies. In particular, with regard to being rewarded by councils for efficiency in operation, little difference exists between respondents in the two types of cities.

The city's budget is the most significant policy statement made by a city council. We asked our respondents to rank the items shown in Table 7.4 as to their importance with the city council in regard to appropriations to departments. The item most frequently cited as most important (cited by 43 percent of respondents) was the amount recommended by the chief executive. The literature on public budgeting and urban politics has indicated that chief executives tend to dominate the budget process and these data confirm those reports.[13] The second most frequently cited item (cited by 25 percent of respondents) was the quality of information supporting departmental requests. The department's effectiveness in accomplishing objectives was ranked first by 10 percent of the respondents, and 7 percent ranked the department's reputation for efficiency as most important. Only 5 percent of the department heads ranked services for the electoral constituents of the departments first. Apparently the impact of incrementalism (the need to continue on-going operations) and the expertise of the professionals (the chief executive and the department heads) tend to reduce the ability of the council to use budget decisions for partisan electoral advantage. Furthermore, constituents tend not to understand the city budget. Ony 2 percent of the departments ranked their clients as having the most effect on the amount their department received from the council. The appropriations process in the city council is not a beehive of interest group activity and influence; anyone who has attended public municipal budget meetings can attest to that. While the budgeting process in the council does not appear to be very politicized, the question being addressed in this chapter is whether a difference exists between reformed and nonreformed cities in the politicization of the process. The data in Table 7.4 provide some answers.

The most striking difference between the two types of cities in the budget process is in the importance of the chief executive's recommendations. City managers clearly have more influence over the city council than do mayors. The manager's influence with the council extends beyond the budget process. The influence is particularly apparent in the lobbying of the council by city departments. In general, departmental lobbying of the council varies greatly between reform cities and nonreform cities. Twenty-one percent of the respondents in the "most reformed" cities reported being very active or at least active in lobbying the council, compared to 48 percent of the department heads in the "most nonreformed" cities. Administrators in municipal reform cities are less likely to lobby the council. The city council chooses chief execu-

Table 7.4. Percentages of City Department Heads' Rankings of Six Factors' Importance in City Council Department Appropriations

| | Factor Importance | | | | | Chief Executive |
| | Rational | | | Political | | |
Degree of Municipal Reform	Quality of Information Provided First or Second	Effectiveness in Accomplishing Objectives First, Second, or Third	Reputation for Efficiency First through Fourth	Strength of Clientele First through Fifth	Services for Constituents First through Fourth	Chief Executive Recommendation First
Most reformed (n=120)	60%	69%	60%	14%	18%	53%
Reformed (n=94)	47%	71%	65%	20%	16%	54%
Nonreformed (n=158)	56%	58%	62%	25%	20%	41%
Most nonreformed (n=157)	46%	57%	62%	29%	32%	32%

Note: Respondents were asked to rank these and one other factor. The rankings included vary according to factor. For example, the percentages for the efficiency factor are the totals of those ranking efficiency as first, second, or third. Rankings shown are those of greatest difference between "most reformed" and "most nonreformed" cities. The factor not in the table is "the prestige of the department"; little difference exists between reform and nonreform cities on this factor.

tives in reform cities, and that fact plus their professional credentials probably encourages the council in such cities to defer to the judgement of the chief executives, especially in a policy area as complicated as the city budget. The major significance of this point in terms of the question being addressed here is that as noted above chief executives in reform cities tend to reward department heads in a more "rational" manner than in nonreform cities.

The data in Table 7.4 indicate a greater politicization of the appropriations process in nonreform cities. Note the differences, for example, between reform cities and nonreform cities in regard to services for electoral constituents and strength of clientele. Department heads from nonreform cities were more likely to rank these items higher than were respondents from reform cities. The items representing a more "rational" approach to budgeting tended to be ranked higher by department heads from reform cities. In particular, respondents from reform cities were more likely to rank higher the importance of the department's effectiveness in accomplishing objectives, and there is a distinctive difference between respondents from the "most reformed" cities and the "most nonreformed" cities with regard to the importance of the quality of information supplied by departments.

The major evidence against the argument that city councils in reform cities tend to be more rational in decision making is the data on the relative importance of efficiency. The data suggest that efficiency is a value as important to city councils in nonreform cities as in reform cities. However, we are not convinced that this is so. If the recommendations of the chief executive is omitted from Table 7.4 and the remaining rankings adjusted for that deletion, differences among the respondents, according to degree of municipal reform, change in regard to the efficiency measure. As indicated in Table 7.5, these adjustments show city councils in the "most reformed" cities to be more favorable to efficiency in determining appropriations than councils in the "most nonreformed" cities. The

Table 7.5. Percentage of City Department Heads' Rankings of Five Factors' Importance in City Council Department Appropriations

	Factor Importance				
	Rational			Political	
Degree of Municipal Reform	Quality of Information First or Second	Effectiveness in Accomplishing Objectives First, Second, or Third	Reputation for Efficiency First through Fourth	Strength of Clientele First through Fourth	Services for Constituents First through Fourth
Most reformed (n=120)	75%	83%	84%	14%	25%
Reformed (n=94)	59%	84%	77%	19%	26%
Nonreformed (n=158)	64%	65%	73%	23%	32%
Most nonreformed (n=157)	52%	67%	68%	24%	35%

Note: The same factors as in Table 7.4 are ranked here except that the rankings for "recommendation of chief executive" are redistributed so that in those instances where that factor was ranked higher than another factor, the latter was raised one ranking in importance. Rankings are those of greatest difference between "most reformed" and "most nonreformed cities." As in Table 7.4, the seventh factor, "prestige of the department," is not given.

adjustments in Table 7.5 in regard to the other factors support the argument that councils in municipal reform cities are more "rational" in their decision making than councils in nonreform cities.

The data in this section support the conclusion that the municipal reform movement and its institutions have made a difference in the attitudes and behavior of city officials. This conclusion rests not on one piece of data, but a general trend running through a variety of data. In the next section we examine other explanations for these findings that might lead to the rejection of such a conclusion.

Other Explanations for Differences

Are the differences in values and behavior noted above between reformed and nonreformed cities the result of the institutions composing our reform scale or are they the consequence of confounding variables? In particular, municipal reform cities differ from nonreform cities in terms of population and geographical location. Differences between respondents from reform cities and nonreform cities may be a function of population or geography. That is, cultural differences associated with geography or size may be the cause of the behavioral differences noted above.

Of cities above 50,000, reform cities tend to be among the smaller in size. Of the respondents from cities between 50,000 and 100,000 (n = 299), 47 percent were from reform cities, compared to 31 percent of those (n = 231) from cities 100,000 and larger. Reform cities also tend to be more common in the West than in the Middle Atlantic states: of the respondents from Connecticut, New Jersey, New York, and Pennsylvania (n = 64), 11 percent were from reform cities; of those respondents from the Mountain and Far Western states (n = 139), 63 percent were from reform cities. Seventy-five percent of the 89 respondents from California were from reform cities. Thus, distinct differences exist between reform and nonreform cities in terms of geography and population. Yet we find no evidence that controlling for these differences changes the conclusions of the previous section.

The data on the perceived objectives of chief executives for respondents from cities under 100,000, are similar to those reported in Table 7.3 for all respondents (see Table 7.6). Similar results can be demonstrated for larger cities. The point being made here is that rational decision making by administrators does not appear to be a function of city size.

Three Western states (Arizona, California, and Washington) offer an opportunity to control for the effects of geography on rational decision making. At least two-thirds of the respondents from each of these states are from municipal reform cities, and each state is represented by at least nine respondents. Thus, the environment of these states seems to favor municipal reform institutions. However, there are a sufficient number of respondents serving in nonreform cities in these states to allow comparison with the respondents from reform cities in a similar geographical location. As can be seen in Table 7.7, the differences reported in Table 7.3 between respondents in reform cities and nonreform cities are still found within this more narrow geographical region. Of course, institutional factors may still not be the reason for these differences; reform and nonreform cities within these three states may differ in culture and this difference may be the reason for the differences found. However, our view is that culture and institutions are both relevant. A longitudinal analysis of attitudes and behavior would be needed to conclude that reform institutions cause more rational decision making. Several studies do support a conclusion that municipal reform institutions can affect voting behavior and electoral outcomes. For example, Eugene Lee's study of nonpartisan elections in California is one such.[14] In any event, officials in reform cities are more rational in their decision making, and our data support the hypothesis that the difference is related to institu-

Table 7.6. Percentages of City Department Heads' Rankings of Departmental Objectives' Importance for City Chief Executive by Degree of Municipal Reform for Cities between 50,000 and 100,000

			Importance*		
Degree of Municipal Reform	Operational Efficiency First or Second	Service Effectiveness First or Second	Service Delivery Equity First, Second, or Third	Maintaining Traditional Services First, Second, or Third	Increasing Service Levels First or Second
Most reformed (n=81)	81%	71%	32%	18%	19%
Reformed (n=61)	70%	74%	33%	31%	24%
Nonreformed (n=76)	63%	79%	20%	30%	32%
Most nonreformed (n=81)	57%	61%	16%	30%	41%

*Respondents were asked to rank these objectives in terms of their importance for their chief executive. Rankings included for each objective are the same as those in Table 7.3.

Table 7.7. Percentages of City Department Heads' Rankings of Departmental Objectives' Importance for City Chief Executive by Degree of Municipal Reform in Three Western States

Degree of Municipal Reform	Operational Efficiency First or Second	Effectiveness of Services First or Second	Importance Service Delivery Equity First, Second, or Third	Maintaining Traditional Services First, Second, or Third	Increasing Service Levels First or Second
Reformed (n=79)	78%	78%	45%	23%	25%
Nonreformed (n=30)	57%	69%	31%	46%	36%

Note: The states are Arizona, California, and Washington.

tional factors rather than such cultural differences as city size or geography.[15]

Even if rational decision making has triumphed in the attitudes and behavior of officials in reform cities, the literature has argued that all is not well in the administration of such cities. If this is so, the real social and political costs of rational decision making may be in fact very high. In particular, Harlan Hahn argues that professionalization of bureaucracies has made them unresponsive to citizens.[16]

Rationality and Responsiveness

The rational approach to administration of reform cities is said to lead to unresponsiveness by administrators to individual citizens' needs, requests, and complaints. In particular, political machines associated with partisan politics and patronage are said to encourage a bureaucracy to be more attuned to the needs of individual citizens. Since bureaucrats' personal future is determined in such political environments by the electoral success of office-holders, they are supposedly encouraged to strive for constituent and client satisfaction. The professionalization of bureaucracy is said to have led bureaucracies to be concerned with professional standards rather than with the needs of clients.[17]

Our data do not support this theory. We asked the city department heads to indicate from a list provided them, what factors are important in their decisions about service delivery and rule enforcement. One of the factors, citizens' requests, suggests a concern for the wants and needs of clients. Fifty-seven percent of the respondents cited this factor. Fifty-one percent of the department heads from the "most reformed" cities (n = 120) cited this factor, compared to 45 percent of those from the "most nonreformed" cities (n = 157). Thus, administrators from municipal reform cities do not appear less concerned about the needs of individual citizens, but rather more so. Furthermore, reform cities administrators' concern for equity in service delivery procedures, noted earlier, suggests a style of administration where all citizens are to be treated fairly.

Not only have municipal reform cities been criticized for being unresponsive to citizens in general, but they have been especially criticized for their tendency to underrepresent minorities. We do not have data on the behavior of city councils and chief executives in regard to their interest in equal treatment, but we do have on city administrators. The literature on urban service delivery suggests that city administrators tend to pay little attention to equality in service delivery but instead use decision rules based on professional norms, objective measures of need, or other rational criteria.[18] As the result of using these standards, urban service delivery is said to be characterized by "unpatterned inequalities" — that is, by inequalities in service delivery that are not intentional.[19]

Presumably, administrators in municipal reform cities, being more concerned with rational values, would place less emphasis on equality in service delivery than administrators from nonreform cities. "Desire for equality" in service delivery and enforcement of regulation was one of the factors listed from which respondents were asked to pick the most important in affecting service delivery and rule enforcement decisions. Thirty-six percent of the department heads checked this factor. Forty-four percent of the respondents from the "most reformed" cities cited it, compared to 34 percent of those from the "most nonreformed" cities. Equality in service delivery is apparently pursued more in reform cities than in nonreform cities.

In summary, citizens and clients fare better in municipal reform cities in the responsiveness of agencies to individual and minority needs. While bureaucracies in nonreform cities may push for more services, the quality of services available may be poorer and the access to services may be more restricted.

Conclusion

Although the data in this chapter tend to indicate that the municipal reform movement has accomplished its objective of encouraging "rational" decision making, we can not ignore the fact that the literature raises serious questions about the positive effects of such decision making in urban government. While we have found criticism about the non-responsiveness to be somewhat incorrect, we recognize the probable validity of other criticisms. Professional administrators probably do tend to treat lower-class clients differently from middle-class clients.[20] Specialization and the use of special purpose governments have tended to make our cities ungovernable. City managers do lack the political base to be the necessary coalition builders in many large and heterogeneous cities. Mayors may feel hemmed in by urban bureaucracies — "the new urban machines."[21] However, not all of these problems are attributable to the municipal reform movement and its institutions. Indeed, the answer to some of these problems probably lies in more reform rather than less.

Chapter 8

Influence of the Chief Executive on City Line Agencies

Studies of the urban chief executive have tended to focus upon either the formal powers of the office,[1] or upon the leadership styles of individual chief executives.[2] Such studies are usually from the perspective of the chief executive. Missing from the literature is information about the chief executive's influence on city line agencies[3] from the perspective of their agency heads. We do not know how agency heads perceive the influence of the chief executive upon them as compared with the influence of other major political actors such as the city council, or interest groups and agency clientele. Similarly, we do not know which factors agency heads regard as most important for the chief executive's ability to influence their agency; nor do we have much information about the consequences of the chief executive's influence for municipal administration. This chapter provides some of the missing information.

The ability or inability of the city chief executive to penetrate the routines of urban administration have significant consequences. The executive reform movement in this century was designed not only to increase popular control over the executive branch, but also to improve the ability of the chief executive to direct and control administrators. Yet, despite the efforts of mayors and city managers to direct and control them, urban administrators exercise a significant amount of discretion.[4] When they use their discretion to serve professional norms or agency goals rather than the wishes of those designated to make policy, control of the bureaucracy by the chief executive may be diminished. The result is policy making by those less accountable to the electorate.[5]

The principal devices that have emerged to facilitate executive leadership in municipal government are: responsibility for and control over the preparation and execution of the budget, power to appoint and remove department heads (the municipal reform movement sought to reduce the number of independently elected agency heads and independent commissions), and the veto (which militates against agency–city council alliances). In essence, the municipal executive reform movement sought to strengthen the executive's administrative powers. As Charles Adrian and Charles Press have reminded us, the weak executive form is "weak" not because the executive lacks policy making powers, but because the executive lacks administrative powers.[6]

Although the municipal executive reform movement concentrated on formal powers, the literature suggests that the informal leadership of chief executives also significantly affects their administrative influence. Richard Neustadt has argued that presidential leadership is a function of the chief executive's ability to persuade others to do his will, and that the ability to persuade is a function of his reputation for accomplishing his objectives.[7] At the state and local levels, studies by Martha Weinberg and by John Kotter and Paul Lawrence demonstrate that executive leadership varies with the individual executive.[8]

This chapter assesses the ability of municipal chief executives (mayors and city managers) to intervene in the administrative process. It begins with a method of measuring executive influence; assesses the effect of formal powers upon the influence of chief executives; examines the effect of leadership style upon influence; compares the relative effect of leadership styles and formal powers on the chief executive's influence; and concludes with an evaluation of the effect of chief executive influence upon administrators. Data for the study were obtained from a mail survey of police, fire, and public works department heads in all cities in the U.S. with a population of 50,000 or more. This survey is described in Chapter 1.

The administrative influence of the chief executive depends in substantial degree upon whether agency heads take into consideration the needs and policy positions of the chief executive when making their own decisions, and whether they perceive the chief executive as being able to affect their dealings with the city council. With these factors in mind, agency heads were categorized according to their responses to the following four measures of chief executive influence:

A. Consideration of the city chief executive's position:

1. The extent to which agency heads consider the policy position of the chief executive in making decisions about service delivery and enforcement of regulations.[9]

2. The extent to which agency heads consider the policy position of the chief executive in responding to requests from council members for services and projects for their districts.[10]

B. Importance of chief executive in agency–city council relations:

3. Relative importance of the chief executive's recommendation in determining the agency's budget appropriation from the council.[11]

4. Importance of chief executive's support for the agency in agency–city council relations.[12]

From these four measures, we computed a cumulative index of chief executive influence in which each of the four items mentioned above was weighted equally. Although the four measures of executive influence were perceived as measuring two separate dimensions of executive influence, the influence index created from them has a coefficient of reproducibility of +.87. Using this index, the factors affecting the influence of the chief executive were examined. A brief examination of the relative influence of the chief executuve will help help establish the significance of this examination.

Executive Primacy and Formal Powers

The executive reform movement sought to enhance the city chief executive's influence and control over municipal line agencies. Our data indicate that municipal department heads regard the chief executive as having more influence on them than does the other major municipal policy maker, the city council. Respondents were asked to compare the chief executive and the city council in terms of impact on departmental programs and objectives. Almost three-fourths (73 percent) of the agency heads reported that the chief executive has greater impact than the council on their activities.[13]

The pattern of executive primacy in large municipalities appears to persist irrespective of the form of city government. In city manager cities (n = 312), 70 percent of the department heads ranked the chief executive first in impact on their agencies; in mayor–council cities (n = 185), 76 percent ranked the chief executive first, as did 73 percent in commission cities (n = 31). Since the chief executive is independently elected in the mayor–council form, it may not be surprising that department heads perceive the mayor as more influential than the council. Somewhat less obvious, however, is the finding that department heads in the council–manager form of government also regard the chief executive as having more impact upon them than the city council, despite the fact that the manager is selected by the council. Apparently, as the literature suggests,[14] the budget preparation powers and expertise of managers make city councils more dependent upon their recommendations than vice versa; and their exercise of management coordination and direction tells the departments that the manager rather than the council is in charge of day-to-day departmental activities. These data suggest that the municipal reform objective of centralizing influence and control in the hands of the chief executive (mayor or city manager) has been accomplished in most large cities. It remains to be seen, however, whether the concentration of formal powers in the hands of the chief executive, rather than dispersing them among the council and independent boards and commissions, actually enables the chief executive to penetrate the municipal bureaucracy so as to control it and give it direction.

The power to propose a budget, to appoint and remove department heads and (for mayors) to veto acts of the city council are the major sources of influence created by the executive reform movement. Although formal powers probably do not in themselves make for a strong institution, such powers are often a prerequisite for significant influence.

Ninety percent of the chief executives in our study are reported by responding city department heads to possess the power to propose the city budget. Since so many of the chief executives have this power, it might be argued that it is actually not very helpful in explaining the influence of chief executives. However, the gamma correlation (+.57) between the influence index and possession of budgetary power indicates that those executives lacking such power are clearly at the lowest levels on the influence index. Another indicator of the importance of the budgetary power for the influence of urban chief executives is the responses of department heads to a question asking them to indicate those factors that lead to the chief executive's having the most influence on them. Seventy-seven percent cited the chief executive's influence on the budget. Clearly the power to propose a budget is an essential power needed to gain influence. Those without it appear to have less influence. However, not all chief executives having the power to propose a budget are equally influential. Other formal powers are important in determining influence.

Approximately eighty percent of the city department head respondents reported that the chief executive in their city possessed the power to appoint most department heads. Theoretically the appointment power enables the chief executive to select department heads who are committed to the same general policy goals and objectives as their chief. Such appointees are believed to be susceptible to the chief executive's influence in matters relating to agency administration.

However, the appointment power, unlike the budgetary power, is usually a nonrecurring exercise of executive authority. Once department heads are appointed, there is a presumption that they will continue in office, often for a tenure of service exceeding that of the chief executive, so long as they carry out their responsibilities in an acceptable manner. Under these circumstances department heads may very well regard factors other than the considerations which led to their initial appointment as being of greater importance in the making of agency decisions (e.g., professionalism or clientele interests). One indication that this may be the case is the fact that only 20 percent of our respondents cited the chief executives' ability to appoint and remove as among the important factors in their ability to influence departmental decisions. Further indication that chief executives cannot be assured of the loyalty of their appointees may be found in the responses of department heads to a question asking them to rank various factors according to importance in determining the size of their budget requests. Sixty-seven percent cited the "program needs" of their departments as most important compared to 16 percent who cited "instructions from the chief executive." Department heads tend to defend the interest of their departments, and this may take priority over the goals of the chief executive.

Table 8.1. City Chief Executive Influence Index by Methods of Selecting Department Head

| Influence Index | Chief executive appointment | Selection | | | |
		Board or commission appointment	Council election	Popular election	Examination
Lowest (n = 135)	70%	22	2	2	5
Low (n = 167)	80%	10	3	0	6
Medium (n = 118)	90%	8	2	1	1
High (n = 66)	89%	8	2	0	2
Highest (n = 36)	92%	3	0	0	6

Percentages do not always total 100% due to rounding.

Yet the appointment power is related to executive influence. The gamma correlation between the influence index and executive appointment power is +.35. Table 8.1 shows that in the two highest categories of executive influence, appointment by the chief executive represents a larger percentage of the total than it does for the two lowest influence categories. The opposite tends to be true for the other methods of selection. When executive influence is low, there is a greater likelihood that department heads are selected by board or commission or some other method.

The overwhelming proportion (82 percent) of department heads included in our survey reported that they are appointed by the chief executive. Although only 4 percent of the agency heads are chosen by examination, it is interesting to note that 81 percent of them are found in the two lowest categories on the executive influence index. When competitive examination is used for selecting municipal department heads, the chief executive is much less likely to be perceived as able to penetrate the professionalized bureaucracy. On balance it appears that those chief executives with the right to appoint department heads may be more influential than those without such power, but as compared to control over budget requests, the power to appoint is reported by respondents to be less important.

Closely related to the power to appoint is the power of removal. Chief executives who possess the power in its broadest form can remove department heads who incur their displeasure. Frequently, however, the chief executive's power of removal is restricted so that removal may only be for "cause." Forty-five percent of the chief executives in our study reported their chief executives possess unrestricted removal powers. As shown in Table 8.2, when two of the principal variations of removal powers are taken into account ("at the pleasure of the chief executive," and "for cause"), removal power is correlated with the executive influence index (+.19).

An examination of Table 8.2 reveals that 59 percent of those city chief executives in the highest influence

Table 8.2. City Chief Executive Influence Index by Power to Remove Department Head

Influence Index	None indicated	Removal Power	
		For cause only	At pleasure
Lowest (n = 146)	21%	44	35
Low (n = 167)	15%	42	44
Medium (n = 124)	10%	46	45
High (n = 69)	8%	45	47
Highest (n = 37)	2%	39	59

Note: Percentages do not always total 100% due to rounding.

Gamma correlation = .19; p < .02. Probability based on chi square.

category possess complete removal power over their agency heads ("at pleasure of the chief executive") and 39 percent possess the power of removal for "cause," while only 2 percent do not possess any removal powers. On the other hand, in the lowest influence category 21 percent of the chief executives do not possess any power of removal as compared with 35 percent who possess complete removal power. It is clear from the data presented in Table 8.2 that possession of removal power does not guarantee a high level of executive influence, but the likelihood of being influential is less among those who do not have removal powers than it is among the chief executives who do.

Most mayors in mayor-council cities possess a veto power; mayors in council-manager cities usually do not; and the fusion of legislative and executive powers in commission cities theoretically precludes the veto. According to our respondents, twenty-seven percent of the chief executives in the survey reported here possess the veto.[15] Although the veto may be an important tool of executive power in dealing with the city council, our data suggest that it is not a very important tool of executive influence over line agencies. The correlation between the executive influence index and possession of the veto is small (gamma = +.13). Another indicator of its unimportance is the perception by department head respondents of their chief executive's ability to influence the council. Only 47 percent of those department heads having chief executives with veto power indicated that the chief executive's ability to influence the council was an important factor in the executive's ability to influence departmental decisions. By comparison, 58 percent of the department heads having chief executives without veto power indicated that the executive's ability to influence the council was an important factor in the executive's ability to influence departmental decisions. If anything, the veto may be a handicap in exerting executive influence over line agencies. To the extent that use of the veto power may produce deadlock between the chief executive and the council, possession of that power may have a deleterious effect on the ability of the executive to influence agency heads.[16] The relationship, then, between the veto power and the executive influence index appears at best to be indirect. Those executives who have the veto usually also have other powers more directly related to executive influence. Since the veto power does not mean much in terms of executive influence over line agencies, we might assume that city managers have just as much influence as mayors with comparable formal powers other than the veto. In fact, managers and mayors have very similar patterns of influence as measured by the index of executive influence.[17]

Leadership Style

The student of urban politics knows from experience that formal powers do not necessarily make city chief executives strong. Some tend to be caretakers and some are activists, and their approaches to the office are reflected in their impact on policy. It is very likely, therefore, that leadership style also makes a difference in the influence of chief executives on city administration.

For chief executives to have an impact on administrative policies, they must make their policy positions clear to administrators. For example, an executive secretary to a governor recently commented to us that department heads frequently call on him to ask about the governor's position. He said that his usual response is for them to do what is right. We suggest that in these kinds of situations the impact of the governor is minimal. Administrators must be able to identify what the chief executive wants in order to do it. Strong chief executives at every level of government communicate to administrators what policies or programs they support.

To determine the extent to which city department heads can identify what their chief executive wants or supports, and to relate this awareness to the influence of the chief executive, department heads were asked to identify, from a list provided, the reasons for their department's support by the chief executive, and these were related to the chief executive influence index. (See Table 8.3). The administrative behavior most supported by chief executives is efficiency in operations. Given the prominent position of chief executives already noted in the budgetary process and recalling the literature on municipal budgeting, which stresses the role of the chief executive as a budget balancer,[18] this concern with efficiency is not surprising. A close second to operational efficiency is executive support for the professionalism of the department's personnel. The combination of efficiency and professionalsim as the two most important values for chief executives suggests the success of the municipal reform movement. Even the next three most frequently supported traits suggest this triumph. Emphasis on program accomplishments, prestige of the department, and objective needs suggest a politically neutral kind of administration.

Other items (see Table 8.3) have more personal connotations. Over a third (35 percent) of the city department heads, for example, identified support of the chief executive's requests as being important in obtaining executive support. Even though a third of the administrators cited this item, the greater frequency with which other items were cited suggests either that chief executives are relatively weak, or that they often fail to communicate their desires, and fail to back up those requests that are communicated with rewards for compliance. It appears that efforts of the municipal reform movement to make city administration more neutral have been more successful than the reformers' efforts to strengthen the chief executive's control of administration.

City chief executives are also concerned about the level of constituent complaints. Almost a third of the agency heads noted that chief executives dislike a high number of constituent complaints. This is somewhat similar to Weinberg's characterization of the governor as a reactor to crises in management.[19]

Table 8.3. City Chief Executive Influence Index by Reasons for Supporting Department

Reason for Chief Executive Support of Agency	Percentage of Department Heads (n = 543)	Reason and Influence Index Correlations (gamma)
Professional		
Operational efficiency	78	+.12
Personnel professionalism	72	+.19
Program accomplishments	65	+.27***
Public prestige of department	49	+.06
Objective needs	36	+.23**
Personal		
Support of chief executive's requests	35	+.39***
Few constituent complaints	31	+.35***
Interest groups and clients' support for department	23	+.17*
Chief executive's political philosophy	14	+.27**
Personal friendship	8	+.39***

*p < .05
**p < .01
***p < .001
Probabilities are based on chi square.

Both professional and personal reasons for chief executive's support are among those positively correlated with the influence index. When administrators can identify what the chief executive supports, the executive's influence is greater. The cumulative index of support, formed by adding the items (see Table 8.3), correlates at +.34 with the index of city chief executive influence.

Of further interest is that the personal items correlate more strongly with the influence index than the professional reasons. City chief executives who reward departments for professional accomplishments do not have as much influence as those executives who reward department heads for their personal and political support. This point illustrates how an emphasis on professionalism in urban administration may undermine the influence of the chief executive. Furthermore, the emphasis placed on professional factors suggests the weakness of chief executives in influencing administrative decision making.

Some city chief executives may fail to communicate to department heads what they want simply because they fail to intervene. The active chief executive is likely to be more influential than the caretaker executive. (See Table 8.4). Department heads were asked to indicate, from a list provided, those things requested by their chief executive in the year prior to the survey. As can be seen in Table 8.4, the chief executives most often requested information. While this finding is anticipated, it nevertheless emphasizes the difficulties for chief executives' trying to influence the decisions of experts in a policy area. In this connection Demetrios Caraley has noted that "the greatest obstacle to the mayor's converting his formal authority as chief executive into full control of the operating departments is not his shortage of legal powers, . . . [It is] his lack of knowledge about . . . more than a tiny fraction of what those departments are doing."[20]

Of particular interest is the fact that over two-thirds of the city agency heads reported being contacted regarding constituent complaints in the year prior to the survey. Again the chief executive as a reactor to crises is suggested. It is instructive to contrast this kind of intervention by the chief executive with the fact that only a third of the department heads reported being called upon to influence patterns of service delivery.

It would, however, be a mistake to understate the city chief executives' intervening with their department heads to influence significant policy matters. A substantial percentage of the administrators reported being contacted concerning the efficiency and effectiveness of their programs and the need for new services. That a third of them

Table 8.4. City Chief Executive Influence Index by Reasons for Calling on Department

Reason	Percentage of Department Heads (n = 543)	Reason and Influence Index Correlations (gamma)
Information	74	.20*
Constituent complaint	68	.30***
Determining need for new or more services	58	.20*
Encouraging coordination	48	.28***
Determining departmental efficiency	48	.19**
Enforcement of laws or regulations	45	.14
Determining effectiveness of policies	41	.20**
Patterns of service delivery	33	.27***
Personnel matter	29	.13
Controlling lobbying of city council.	5	.08

*p < .05
**p < .01
***p < .001
Probabilities are based on chi square.

were called about patterns of service delivery and 45 percent were called upon with regard to enforcement of laws and regulations suggests that chief executives are often more than just caretakers needing information or crisis managers responding to constituent complaints and personnel problems. Of particular importance is that 48 percent of the agency heads reported being called about coordination with other departments. It will be recalled that one of the main goals of the municipal executive reform movement was to strengthen the chief executive so as to secure greater departmental coordination.

Regardless of what urban chief executives seek when they contact their department heads, doing so is correlated positively with the executive influence index. (See Table 8.4). Chief executives who do intervene tend to have more influence than other chief executives. Interestingly, intervention regarding constituent complaints, coordination among departments, and service delivery patterns are the most strongly correlated with the influence index. Chief executives who intervene for these reasons, tend to have more influence, as measured by the index, than chief executives concerned with efficiency and effectiveness. These findings are consistent with the data on executive influence and reasons for executive support of departments (see Table 8.3).

Determinants of Influence

In the two preceding sections three formal powers and two leadership styles were found to affect urban chief executive influence. In this section we seek to determine which of these independent variables contributes the most to explaining variation in the influence index. In order to do so, three indices were computed. First, an index of formal powers was calculated from those variables (power to propose a budget, and to appoint and remove the respondent regardless of reason) found to be most closely related to the index. Second, an index of chief

Table 8.5. Combinations of Three City Chief Executive Relationships with Departments by Influence Index

| | | | | Relationship Combinations | | | | |
	Type I	Type II	Type III	Type IV	Type V	Type VI	Type VII	Type VIII
	(n^e=64) (n^o=84)	(n^e=101) (n^o=107)	(n^e=69) (n^o=59)	(n^e=39) (n^o=31)	(n^e=64) (n^o=91)	(n^e=41) (n^o=40)	(n^e=62) (n^o=43)	(n^e=105) (n^o=90)
Influence Index								
Lowest	8%	18%	18%	27%	50%	38%	32%	31%
Low	28	27	32	33	37	28	33	30
Medium	23	30	29	27	11	24	23	20
High	22	19	15	5	3	6	6	14
Highest	19	6	6	8	0	4	6	5
Total	100%	100%	100%	100%	101%	100%	100%	100%

Notes: Chief executive combinations:

Type I — strong formal powers, strong intervention, strong personal relations;
Type II — weak formal powers, strong intervention, strong personal relations;
Type III — strong formal powers, weak intervention, strong personal relations;
Type IV — strong formal powers, strong intervention, weak personal relations;
Type V — weak formal powers, weak intervention, weak personal relations;
Type VI — strong formal powers, weak intervention, weak personal relations;
Type VII — weak formal powers, strong intervention, weak personal relations;
Type VIII — weak formal powers, weak intervention, strong personal relations;

"Strong" refers to respondents reporting their chief executive above the median in each index.

Using chi square, the respective probabilities of the distribution in Types II, III, and IV with respect to the distribution of Type I are less than .05, as are the respective probabilities for Types VI, VII, and VIII in relation to Type V.

"n^o" refers to expected frequency and "n^o" to observed frequency of each type.

executive intervention was calculated by adding the reasons cited by each respondent for their chief executive's intervention in their department (see Table 8.4). Finally, an index of personal reasons for executive support was calculated from the items listed (see the second part of Table 8.3). Each index was divided near the median so as to apportion the respondents according to strong and weak formal powers, intervention and personal contact. The resulting six parts were then combined into eight chief executive types. (See Table 8.5).

The data show that all three indices contribute to explaining the variation of the dependent variable, city chief executive influence. For example, in Types II, III, and IV, the presence of one weak characteristic (a different one in each type) results in lower executive influence compared to Type I executives who are strong on all three indices. Thus, each of the indices makes an independent contribution to explaining the influence of the chief executive.

The index measuring personal relations in executive support is shown by the data (see Table 8.5) to indicate that such ties have the most impact of the three variables. Weakness in this characteristic, in Type IV, reduces influence more sharply than weakness in the other characteristics, in Types II and III, and strength in this characteristic, in Type VIII, increases influence more than strength in the other characteristics, as in Types VI and VII.

The reader should be cautious in interpreting the observed frequencies of each type. Because each index could not be divided into halves, the expected frequencies for each type was not the same. (Differences in the expected frequencies are included in Table 8.5.) It is of interest that significantly higher than expected observed frequencies occurred in the two symmetrical types, I and V, where the three characteristics were either all high or all low. These three indices are positively correlated. Thus, there is a tendency for chief executives strong in one characteristic to be strong in both of the other two.

Consequences of Influence

At least three consequences might be expected to follow from the reported patterns of city chief executive influence. First, those urban agency heads most affected by chief executive intervention would perceive themselves as having less discretion than other administrators. Second, chief executive influence would constitute a threat to administrative neutrality. Third, where the chief executive is strong, agency heads would be more dependent on the chief executive.

As indicated in Table 8.6, the relationship between city chief executive influence and the discretion of urban agency heads in patterns of service delivery — which areas of the city get what services — suggests that the influence of the chief executive does have significant policy implications. As expected, agency heads with an influential chief executive are more likely to perceive themselves as having less discretion in service delivery. Nevertheless, a large amount of discretion apparently

Table 8.6. City Chief Executive Influence Index by Discretion in Patterns of Service Delivery

		Discretion	
	Total	Great deal	Some or none
Influence Index			
Lowest (n = 122)	46%	43	11
Low (n = 143)	42%	48	10
Medium (n = 112)	34%	49	17
High (n = 62)	27%	58	15
Highest (n = 34)	18%	44	38

Note: The respondents were asked the following question: "How much discretion does your department have in regard to patterns of service delivery (which areas of the city get what services)?"

Gamma correlation = .23

x^2 = 29.0, p < .002

remains for department heads even with strong chief executives.

Does the influence of the chief executive in limiting the discretion of administrators threaten administrative neutrality? The goal of administrative neutrality is to ensure fairness in procedures and service delivery. The responses of the city department heads give little indication that executive intervention ordinarily presents a management problem. In fact, just 9 percent reported that intervention by the chief executive presented such a problem. Furthermore, executive intervention is seldom for the purpose of favoritism. Only 6 percent of the respondents indicated that in the year prior to the survey the chief executive had sought to use their department to reward constituents. Strong chief executives do not engage in this kind of intervention any more than other chief executives. Although some observers may believe that intervention by any chief executive for the purpose of favoritism is too high, the conclusion must be that from the perspective of city department heads executive influence does not represent a significant threat to their neutrality.

A third consequence of the influence of the chief executive over administration is that agency heads under a strong executive tend to go to the chief executive for assistance. A strong chief executive is particularly helpful to agencies in their relations with the external environment. As indicated in Table 8.7, department heads under strong chief executives rely on them more than do other department heads for assistance with the city council, officials in other governments, and interest groups. Of course, the strong chief executive may require agency heads to relate to the external environment through the executive office. The strong chief executive probably welcomes this broker relationship.

Implications

Unlike state government, the question of who has more influence over city executive branch agencies, the

Table 8.7. City Chief Executive Influence Index by Reasons Department Heads Contacted Chief Executive

	Percentage of Department Heads (n = 543)	Correlation Between Influence Index and Reasons for Contacting Chief Executive (gamma)
Reason		
Support before city council	46	.28**
Support with other governments	24	.34**
Aid with interest groups	12	.33**
Interagency coordination	27	.15
Building public support	27	.11
Justifying existing programs	49	.14*
Program expansion	68	.07

*p < .02
**p < .001
Probabilities are based on chi square.

chief executive or the legislative body, has been resolved in favor of the chief executive. However, this may be more the result of the weakness of the city council than of the influence of the mayor or the city manager. We know that the effort of the municipal executive reform movement to give chief executives formal powers to influence urban administration has been successful. Nevertheless, we also know that formal powers are not in themselves enough to gain control of administration; leadership style is also an important consideration. Those executives who have power and who seek to use it are apparently able to make a difference in the behavior of their department heads.

A final caveat is necessary. The findings in this chapter have been based on only three municipal line agencies. The applicability of such findings to other departments of municipal government remains open to speculation. The departments included in this study are three of the oldest and most established agencies found in city government. In this respect they differ from the new community development and social service agencies which have been established to administer federal grant programs. The bureaucratic routines of police, fire, and public works departments may be more difficult for department heads and chief executives to penetrate than those of newer agencies. Yet the state administration literature suggests that agencies supported by federal grants are also difficult for the chief executive and legislature to control.[21] However, special revenue sharing, which tends to undermine intergovernmental administrative linkages, may turn out to make such agencies more vulnerable to local chief executive control.

An earlier version of this chapter appeared in *Public Administration Review*, Volume 42, No. 2 (March/April 1982).

Chapter 9

Council Intervention in Municipal Administration

Traditionally, city councils have been involved in administration. During the nineteenth century the weak executive form of government was the most common arrangement for decision making at the local level. This pattern has continued right up to the present in counties and smaller cities of the nation. In this form of government, departments are run by executives elected to their position by the voters, council committees, or boards. In each instance the powers of the chief executive over administration are weak and the influence of the council is great. In the twentieth century, two efforts were made to reduce the influence of the city council in administration. First, the executive reform movement sought to modernize administration by increasing the administrative power of the chief executive and by professionalizing management in the executive branch. Second, the municipal reform movement sought to get politics out of city government by making all its components, including the city council, less partisan. This was attempted through the introduction of the merit system in personnel selection and promotion, and the use of nonpartisan and at-large elections.

In spite of these efforts, city council involvement in municipal administration has continued. The reform movements did not attempt to divest city councils of their important legislative oversight duties, and constituent casework continues to be an important task for legislators at all levels of government. Service to constituents often requires council members to call upon administrators for information and assistance in dealing with constituent complaints and requests. Such council intervention may threaten the neutrality of administrative decision making sought by the reform movement, and it may undermine the authority of the chief executive sought by the executive reform movement.[1] There is, however, a paucity of information in the literature on local government about the extent to which constituent casework leads to intervention by council members in city administration and about the consequences of that intervention. Specifically, we do not know if it threatens the neutrality of administrators, or leads to council control over administrative decision making. Further, we do not know much about the benefits that administrators derive from such intervention, nor how reform institutions have affected the frequency and consequences of council intervention. This chapter seeks to supply that information from the perspective of municipal department heads.[2] The data were obtained from a mail survey of police, fire, and public works department heads in all cities in the United States with a population of 50,000 or more. This survey is described in Chapter 1.

Council Requests

The literature on municipal administration frequently cites a communication gap between the bureaucracy and the citizenry.[3] Our data indicate that council members serve as communication links for their constituents across this gap.[4] Respondents were asked to indicate how often they had been contacted by council members during the year preceding the survey about six items (shown in Table 9.1). As indicated by the data, council requests are not

Table 9.1. City Council Member Requests to City Departments

Reason	Percentage of Department Heads Receiving at Least One Request (n=510)				Median Number of Requests
	Total	Fire	Police	Public Works	
Information	65	67	64	64	5.5
Complaints	63	41	68	81	10.0
Regulations affecting constituents	53	45	44	68	7.3
Projects or services for district	44	34	44	54	8.2
Jobs for constituents*	14	14	7	21	4.5
Contracts for constituents	8	4	6	13	5.3

Note: Excluded are those respondents who were unable or unwilling to specify either numbers or contact. Thirty-three or about 6 percent of the respondents did not respond to this question.

*Percentages are slightly higher for Northeastern cities.

daily matters in the life of a municipal department head, but neither are they atypical.

City council members contact municipal department heads for three basic reasons: to obtain information about departmental programs, to represent the interests of constituents in matters related to departmental services, and to seek special treatment by the department for their constituency or individual constituents. Council members' intervention is of an "informant" type whenever they contact department personnel for information about departmental programs. Such requests may, for example, be on behalf of constituents seeking information about eligibility for employment with the public works department, the frequency of police patrols, or the availability of fire prevention information. Such requests are typically regarded by the department as routine and are easily complied with by supplying information readily available to departmental personnel. A single encounter is usually all that is necessary to satisfactorily deal with the request. As indicated in Table 9.1, sixty-five percent of all department heads reported having at least one such request (more than one in most cases) from a council member during the year preceding the survey. The level of council intervention of this type was almost the same for fire, police,and public works departments.

City council intervention is of a "mediator" type whenever council members contact municipal departments to discuss departmental regulations affecting their constituents, or to report constituent complaints about departmental services. Although routine inquiries about departmental regulations are essentially requests for information, council member contacts for discussing departmental regulations may place the council member in a mediating position between constituent and municipal department. The restaurant operator who has been warned by the fire prevention inspector to bring his kitchen equipment into conformity with the fire safety code, or the merchant whose customers are being ticketed for parking violations while they patronize his store, are examples of the kinds of constituents who may seek council aid in obtaining clarification (and perhaps a degree of nonenforcement) of departmental policies regarding city ordinance enforcement. Fifty-three percent of the department heads responding to our questions reported at least one contact during the year preceding the survey by city council members for the purpose of discussing agency regulations. The frequency of contact for this purpose was considerably higher in public works departments than in fire or police departments.

Council members also perform a mediator role when they bring constituent complaints about service delivery to the attention of the municipal department. Complaints about delays on the part of police or fire departments in responding to calls, or about the frequency of road repairs and the quality of waterline maintenance are all examples of the kinds of constituent complaints that lead to council member contacts with department administrators. On some occasions council members may conclude rather quickly that the constituent complaint is unfounded or the result of a misunderstanding. On other occasions, however, the council member may attempt to mediate the contending positions of the constituent and the department. Sixty-three percent of the department heads reported contacts in which complaints about service delivery were involved. As indicated in Table 9.1, apparently fire departments are less likely to receive complaints through city council members about service delivery than either police or public works departments, while public works departments are most likely to receive complaints. This is not especially surprising when we consider the kinds of services provided by each of the departments. Because there is likely to be less departmental discretion involved in the delivery of fire-fighting services than there is in the performance of public works activities, city council members are likely to be called upon to intervene with public works officials more often than with fire officials.

A third type of intervention performed by council members is that of "procurer" of services. This procurement function has at least two dimensions: the general request for additional municipal services in the council member's district, and the request for either jobs or contracts for particular constituents. Forty-four percent of the department heads reported being contacted for more services for council districts. While a request for a more favorable (and probably disproportionate) allocation of services for a council district may result in a slight distortion of departmental priorities, it is not likely to be viewed in the same way as the request for preferential treatment in the awarding of contracts (for example for equipment) or in personnel selection. Fourteen percent of the municipal department heads reported having been contacted during the past year for jobs for constituents of individual council members; and eight percent also reported having been contacted about the awarding of contracts. Although these percentages are considerably lower than the level of contacts for other purposes, they are surprisingly high in view of the widespread practice in large cities of selecting municipal personnel according to competitive procedures and the use of competitive bidding in the awarding of purchase contracts. As can be seen from Table 9.1, this activity is much more prevalent in the case of public works departments. The distributive nature of the services[5] and the higher incidence of contract work performed by those departments, as well as the likelihood that their work force is less professionalized, partially account for the greater degree of this type of council intervention with public works departments. It should also be pointed out that the incidence of council member requests for district projects or services and jobs for constituents is somewhat higher in the cities of the Northeast. However, as we will subsequently see, the frequency of those forms of council intervention is greater in nonreform cities of the Northeast than in the reform cities of that region — a pattern which pertains to the country as a whole irrespective of region.

As noted earlier, the municipal reform movement sought to minimize the intrusion of partisan politics in the conduct of administration. It did not, however, seek to curtail the important function of legislative oversight through which administrative agencies could be held accountable for the performance of their duties. Of the three types of council member intervention identified, the informant mode is the most compatible with the goal of administrative neutrality envisioned by the municipal reform movement. The mediator type is somewhat less consistent with that objective. Although receiving complaints about service delivery and discussing regulations with council members may aid administrators in making needed program adjustments, these acts of intervention can easily lead to bargaining; and for the reformers administrative decisions were to be guided by rational, objective standards and not by negotiations. More clearly inconsistent with the standards of the reformers are interventions of the "procurement" type. These acts are clearly designed to encourage particularism in administrative decision making, a form of activity which Emmette Redford has characterized as "micropolitics."[6]

In order to determine if the executive and municipal reform movements had their intended impact on the patterns of council intervention in municipal administration, reform cities were compared with nonreform cities for each of the intervention categories. The principal devices used by reformers to reduce the influence of particularistic concerns and to enhance the influence of general interests, were the city manager form, and nonpartisan and at-large elections. The city manager form promoted governance by professional administrators rather than by political brokers while nonpartisan and at-large elections were aimed at producing a legislative branch that would tend toward consideration of the interests of the whole community over partisan or particularistic interests.

As can be seen from Table 9.2, the most pronounced difference between reform and nonreform cities is found in

Table 9.2. Types of City Council Members' Requests to City Departments by Degree of Municipal Reform

Intervention Role	Reason	City Manager (n=305)	Mayor–Council or Commission (n=211)	At-large Elections (n=279)	Ward and Mixed Elections (n=231)	Low Party Activity (n=235)	High Party Activity (n=273)
Informant	Information	59%	73%	64%	66%	62%	67%
Mediator	Complaints	62	66	60	68	66	62
	Regulations affecting constituents	48	60	46	61	48	56
Procurer	Projects or services for districts*	36	56	32	59	36	52
	Jobs for constituents*	8	22	9	20	9	19
	Contracts for constituents	6	10	7	8	6	10

Note: Data presented in this table somewhat understate the impact of municipal reform institutions on council member intervention in police and public works departments, and somewhat overstate the impact on intervention in fire departments. Council impact has been greater on police and public works departments than on fire departments.

*Although the percentages in these categories are slightly higher for Northeastern cities, the difference persists between reform and nonreform cities for each of the three institutions of municipal reform.

procurer intervention. On each of the three dimensions of reform (council–manager versus mayor–council and commission forms, at-large elections versus ward and mixed elections, and low versus high party activity),[7] department heads report a higher degree of procurer activity in nonreform than in the reform cities. This is the expected pattern, since one of the goals of the municipal reform movement was to reduce political influence "in the sense of a competitive struggle . . . for private advantages."[8] It attempted to eliminate the practice of promising public jobs in return for electoral support, and it sought to replace the practice of awarding contracts on the basis of favoritism and partisan advantage with a system of competitive bidding.

In contrast, there are not substantial differences between reform cities and nonreform cities in the informant type of intervention. In both reform and nonreform cities the council is made up of part-time amateurs, while administrators are full-time professionals who possess the information which council members need to perform their casework and oversight duties. Legitimate council requests for information are not likely to be viewed by professional administrators as threatening to their neutral competence. It would have been surprising to have found large differences between city types in the frequency of this form of council intervention.

There appears not to be a great deal of difference between reform and nonreform cities in the amount of council member intervention with complaints about service delivery. Reform cities, however, are somewhat less likely than nonreform cities to have council intervention to discuss regulations affecting constituents. Probably this type of intervention is more threatening to administrative neutrality than is the relaying of complaints about service delivery. In a legal sense, variation in service delivery is certainly more tolerable than is the lack of uniformity in regulations and their enforcement. Reform institutions apparently do minimize those types of council intervention that are most threatening to administrative neutrality.

Consequences of Council Intervention

The effects of city council members' intervention may be investigated from three perspectives: its perceived effects on administrative policy making, on management and managerial decisions about regulation and service delivery, and on liaison with the city council. Both positive and negative consequences of such intervention can be identified.

According to the municipal reform literature, there are several potential negative consequences. First, council intervention may undermine the efforts of the reformers to place the administrative function in the hands of professional administrators and the legislative function in the hands of the council. Intervention may threaten the prerogatives of the administrator and make his ability to perform efficiently and effectively quite difficult. Second, council intervention may affect the management of an agency, particularly with regard to the morale of personnel. Favoritism resulting from council member requests may undermine the professionalism of department personnel. Third, such intervention may be problematical for administrators in their relationships with the city council. Although the reform movements encouraged professionalism in governmental administration, they did not remove city councils from their central roles as policy makers. By emphasizing civil service and professionalism, the reform movements have probably produced administrators who are less capable than their predecessors in dealing with elected officials who have needs and values quite different from their own. If administrators come to view council intervention as an attack on their professionalism, ill feeling engendered toward the council may in turn harm administrators in their subsequent efforts to gain council support for their programs.

From the perspective of the municipal reform movements, the intervention of council members is likely to be viewed as posing a threat to good administration. However, from a pragmatic as well as from a theoretical perspective, council interventions also afford administrators opportunities in policy making, management, and liaison with the city council.

City council intervention may encourage administrators to follow the policy leadership of the council. Improvements in the quality of municipal administration have not been accompanied by a corresponding development in the quality of city council members. As a result, councils have often either delegated their policy-making powers to administrators or allowed them to be assumed by default. The amateurism of city councils discourages the use of legislative oversight as a device for holding administrators accountable to the policies of the council. Intervention may be a substitute, albeit a weak one, for the inability of councils to perform this aspect of their jobs. Therefore, council intervention may be a proxy for fulfilling an important principle of democratic theory — that those who make policy should be those who are accountable to the electorate. Of course, those administrators who are more concerned with management efficiency than with political accountability may view such influence as a disadvantage.

While city council intervention may harm the morale of personnel, it may also serve as a check on the staff. A difficulty faced by virtually all department heads is how to obtain information on the performance of agency personnel. This is an especially important concern in police departments where, as James Q. Wilson points out,[9] discretion tends to be greater rather than less in the lower levels of the organization. The ombudsman-like role played by council members in doing their constituent casework provides opportunities for the department head to obtain feedback about the quality of his staff and his programs.

A further advantage of city council intervention is that it provides an opportunity for communication between administrators and the city council. The amateurism of the council often contributes to a lack of understanding of administrative problems and needs. Intervention provides an opportunity for administrators to educate council members, and perhaps more important to build support for their programs in the council. As long as budget appropriations and program authorizations are the responsibility of the council, administrators are well served in taking advantage of every intervention opportunity to lobby the council.

It is clear that city council intervention may have both positive and negative consequences for municipal department heads. Those consequences will now be explored in greater detail.

Department Heads as Policy Makers

City councils often cast policy statements in rather general terms, recognizing that administrators will extend, refine, and interpret those statements with implementation regulations of their own. A potential consequence of council intervention is to produce mid-course adjustments in agency regulations to make them correspond more closely to the original policy statements of the council. However, only 16 percent of the department heads perceive this to be an advantage resulting from their council contacts. Municipal department heads may not perceive the council as having very definite policy standards with which they need to be in accord, or they may believe they are already in accord with council policies, or they may not desire to be in accord with council policy. Whatever the case, municipal department heads do not perceive council members' intervention as very useful as a policy coordination mechanism.

Council intervention may also have an impact on departmental policy priorities. Thirty-two percent of the respondents (slightly higher for public works departments) perceived contacts by council members on behalf of constituents to result in a distortion of their priorities. It is, of course, significant that approximately a third of the department heads view council member contacts as having negative policy consequences for their agency. The ideal of a professionally competent, neutral administrator conducting the affairs of his agency in the interest of the whole community has long been a goal of the municipal reform movement. (In contrast, the policy concerns of council members have been frequently characterized as parochial.) Council intervention, particularly of the procurer type, represents a violation of administrative neutrality. However, it is perhaps even more significant that only 32 percent of the respondents perceived council intervention to be problematical for departmental priorities. This is perhaps explained by the greater frequency of informant and/or mediator contacts, which tend to be less threatening to the professionally determined priorities of the department. It may also reflect the department heads' perceptions of the relative weakness of council members to influence their departmental priorities. When asked to compare the city council, the chief executive, and interest groups according to which had the greatest impact on their programs, only 26 percent of the department heads said that the council had the greatest impact; most identified the chief executive as having the greatest impact.

Department Heads as Managers

In addition to being a policy maker, the municipal department head is also the manager of an organization that regulates public conduct, protects the public safety, and delivers public services. Department heads were asked to select from a variety of alternatives the most serious management problem they faced as a department head. Interference with departmental policy by council members was selected by 10 percent of the respondents. Thirty-seven percent of the department heads indicated that requests from council members are important in their decisions about the patterns of service delivery and enforcement of regulations; 21 percent thought it led to partiality in service delivery; and 18 percent said it led to lack of strict adherence to departmental regulations. Public works department heads were more likely to perceive council intervention as leading to partiality in service delivery (31 percent) and to lack of strict adherence to departmental regulations (28 percent) than either of the other two types of department heads.

Some indication of the impact of this interference emerges when we find that 29 percent of all municipal department heads indicated that requests from council members on behalf of constituents harmed the morale of departmental personnel. That finding is not especially surprising. The model of professionalism that emerged from the municipal reform movement implies a professional (rather than clientele) determination of which services and regulations are necessary and appropriate for clients. Morale may very well be negatively affected when administratively established priorities and professionally determined standards are compromised by political intercession.

Unfortunately we are unable to determine from our data whether the perceived harm to city department morale is the result of specific council requests for special treatment of constituents or simply a more generalized resentment on the part of department professionals that council members are able to intrude upon what they believe to be professional prerogatives. If as Harlan Hahn suggests,[10] a legacy of the municipal reform movement has been to place more emphasis on the training and qualifications of public service providers than on the satisfaction or dissatisfaction of clients receiving services, it is understandable that some administrators view intervention on behalf of dissatisfied constituents as a serious management problem.

Although council intervention is perceived by department heads as having harmful consequences for departmental morale, they also report that it can be a useful feedback mechanism through which management can learn about problems that may be developing for departmental programs and personnel. Thirty-seven percent of our respondents indicated that they have been able to improve the quality of their service and regulation through information conveyed to them by council members. This would suggest that council members are functioning as surrogate ombudsmen for municipal administration.

Liaison with the Council

Despite their negative feelings about council intervention, municipal department heads recognize the importance of the council's support for their programs. Council intervention is not a one-way communication. Department heads recognize it as an opportunity to educate the council about their programs. Seventy percent of the department heads reported that council contacts have the advantage of enabling them to provide information to the council about what they do. The more knowledge the council has about departmental achievements and strengths, and the more it is aware of agency problems and needs, the greater the likelihood that it will support departmental programs. Thirty-two percent of the department heads said that council intervention has worked to their advantage in increasing support in the council for their programs, while only 6 percent reported that such contacts hurt their support with the council. Apparently departments are not hurt in the council by constituent complaints so long as council members are satisfied with the responses they receive when they contact the department on behalf of constituents. Further evidence of departmental awareness of the importance of council members' support can be seen from the fact that 14 percent of the department heads indicated that when they lobby the city council they deliberately seek out council members whose constituents benefit from their activities.

Although municipal department heads may prefer that individual council members not bother them, they cannot avoid nor should they underestimate the importance of contacts with the city council. Despite the separation of the legislative and executive branches, administration is not divorced from council politics.

Consequences and Reform

We have examined how the municipal reform movement has affected the frequency of council intervention in the administration of the cities included in this study. Reform cities tended to have less intervention than non-reform cities and to have intervention characterized by fewer attempts at what we called "procurement." In this section we examine the effects of the reform movement from intervention when it does occur.

Using the three institutions of the reform movement in Table 9.2, we constructed a municipal reform index in which all items were weighted equally. We then compared the differences in intervention consequences cited by municipal department heads according to this index. Because department heads in cities with little intervention tend to perceive very few consequences resulting from intervention, we restricted our examination to only those cases (n = 354) where the department had been contacted for at least two of the reasons shown in Table 8.1. 9.1

There is little difference in the perceptions of municipal administrators with regard to most of the consequences. However, two differences do emerge. First, the department heads from reform cities are more likely to see the major advantage of such intervention to be the opportunity to educate the city council about the programs of their departments. Of the department heads from the "most reformed" cities (n = 74), 83 percent cited this as an advantage, compared to 65 percent of those department heads from the "least reformed" cities (n = 67). In his study of city managers, R.O. Loveridge argued that these administrators place a high value on educating the members of the council about the problems of the city and about the proper role of council and administrators in council–manager cities.[11] Apparently, this orientation carries over to other administrators in reform cities. Since on many of our measures department heads in reform cities are not more likely to perceive advantages and are not less likely to perceive harm from intervention, we might conclude that the education process is not very effective. Nevertheless, there is a second difference in their perceptions which suggests that administrators in reform cities may be under less pressure from council intervention.

The manner in which city council members' intervention is handled seems to have more effect on how well departments fare with councils in nonreform cities than in reform cities. For example, from a list of seven factors affecting the budgeting decisions of city councils, 38 percent of the department heads from the nonreform cities selected their response to council requests as one of the four most important factors affecting departmental budgetary success, while only 20 percent of the department heads from the "most reformed" cities selected it as among the most important factors. Seven percent of the department heads from the nonreform cities said that council intervention hurt their support in the council, while only two percent of the department heads from the "most reformed" cities viewed intervention as harmful. Furthermore, department heads from the reform cities were less likely to see their responses to council intervention as increasing support in the council for their legislative proposals. Forty-six percent of the department heads from the nonreform cities saw it as helping their legislative proposals, compared to 22 percent of the heads from the "most reformed" cities. The pattern is clear. Department heads have to be more cautious in dealing with intervention in the nonreform cities than in the reform cities. Although the perceived consequences for management do not seem to differ between the two types of cities, the legislative consequences appear to be significantly different. The manner in which council intervention is handled seems to have less effect on council support in the reform cities.

One interpretation of this pattern might be that city councils are just not as important in reform cities as in nonreform cities. Perhaps city managers are able to dominate councils so much that they tend to follow the leadership of the manager. However, our data suggest that city councils have more influence in reform cities than they do in nonreform cities. Respondents were asked to indicate which of the following three actors has the most impact on their programs: the chief executive, the city council, or *enhancing central authority of council?*

interest groups. Forty-two percent of the department heads in the "most reformed" cities identified the council as the most important actor, compared to 18 percent of the heads from the nonreform cities.

Even though department heads in reform cities regard the council as important to the success of their programs, it may still be the case that those administrators need to worry less about offending the council because they are able to lead the council. In dealing with members of the city council, administrators in reform cities are able to invoke the aura of municipal reform to educate the council about the significance of professionalism and neutrality in administration. This may give them an advantage in influencing the city council. Somewhat supporting this explanation are the 17 percent of the department heads from the nonreform cities who said that council intervention made their administrative decisions correspond more closely with the policies of the city council, while only 11 percent of the heads from the "most reformed" cities cited this. Department heads in reform cities may have a greater ability to remain independent of the council because of their ability to influence it.

Conclusion

A major objective of the executive and municipal reform movements was to reduce the influence of the city council in administration. These reform movements were successful in strengthening the chief executive and in professionalizing departmental personnel. However, council members' intervention in administration on behalf of constituents is still common. Nevertheless, the evidence we have presented suggests that the reform institutions have skewed the nature of the intervention in such a manner as to support the reform objective of neutrality in municipal administration. In particular, the evidence suggests that intervention aimed at acts of favoritism is found more often in nonreform cities than in reform cities. Furthermore, because they are able to use the occasions of council intercession to educate the council members, municipal department heads in reform cities are apparently less likely to perceive intervention as threatening to their overall legislative relationships.

The municipal reform movements have been criticized frequently as having created, in their pursuit of neutrality, a communication gap between administrators and their clientele. Our investigation suggests that the reform movements have not significantly affected the information function performed by administrators in responding to council intervention — a function that is probably valuable in reducing the communication gap between them. While council intervention continues to provide information, the reform institutions have apparently worked to reduce the neutrality threatening aspects of this contact. In short, the reform institutions appear to have been successful in bringing about neutrality in municipal administration without incurring the problems of estrangement from clientele so often associated with them in the literature.

An earlier version of this chapter appeared in *Administration and Society*, Volume 13, No. 4 (February 1982).

Chapter 10

Interest Group Influence in City Policy Making: The Views of Administrators

The influence of interest groups on the formulation and implementation of public policies in American cities is a much debated matter. The discussion has often centered on whether the pattern of influence is pluralistic, involving many interest groups, or elitist, confined to a particular group such as a business or economic elite.[1] Sometimes, the discussion has focussed on the responsiveness of elected city officials.[2] The proximity of council members to their constituents is said to make them more responsive to interest groups than legislators at any other level.[3] Yet several features of the municipal reform movement are believed to have made city governments somewhat resistant to interest group influence.[4] (For a contrary view, see David J. Greenstone and Paul E. Peterson,[5] and Alana Northrop and William H. Dutton[6].) The truth is that not much is known about how interest groups influence local government policy. This chapter seeks to add to our limited knowledge by examining the influence of interest groups on city policy making from the perspective of the heads of three traditional line agencies in city government.

Municipal department heads are a valuable source of information about interest group influence. Because department heads play an important role in the formulation and implementation of policies,[7] they represent an important point of potential access for interest groups seeking to influence programs. Furthermore, these administrators' interactions with the city council and the chief executive officer provide a unique view of the influence of interest groups on city leaders.

The linkage between interest group influence and government administration has always been a somewhat tenuous one. On the one hand, interest groups have been viewed as appropriate vehicles for aggregating and articulating the interests of an agency's constituents. In this respect, interest groups function as a form of popular representation that complements the electoral process. The administrative agency–interest group linkage which J. Leiper Freeman,[8] A. Lee Fritschler,[9] and Emmette S. Redford[10] have characterized as "subsystem politics" is widely recognized in the study of American politics and administration. On the other hand, interest group activity may constitute a form of particularism that leads to special advantage in the distribution of agency services, and special privilege in the enforcement of agency regulations. The balancing act is one of ensuring that interest groups will be afforded sufficient access to administrative agencies so that they may be able to articulate their positions, while at the same time ensuring that interest group activity is adequately restricted so as to protect the neutrality of administrative decision making. It is in this context that we are especially interested in the perceptions of city department heads regarding the consequences of interest group activities.

Our discussion will begin with an analysis of the perceptions of these respondents regarding the influence of interest groups in their respective policy areas. Then we shall investigate which types of groups have influence and how they gain access to decision making. Finally, we will examine from the perspective of the department heads consequences they perceive from interest group influence. The data were obtained from a mail survey of police, fire and public works department heads in all cities in the United States with a population of 50,000 or more described in Chapter 1.

Group Influence

Interest groups do not dominate decision making in the cities. As seen in Table 10.1, less than a quarter of the respondents reported that interest groups have a great deal of influence in their policy areas. However, interest groups are not a neglible factor. Only fifteen percent of the respondents reported that interest groups have little or no influence. These data show interest groups to have more influence in the policy areas of public works and police than fire.

While interest groups are influential in the making of city policy, they certainly do not dominate that process at the expense of elected officials. From the perspective of the city department heads, the chief executive and the city

Table 10.1. Extent of Interest Group Effects on Policy Reported by Various City Department Heads

Extent of Effect	Percentage of Department Heads			
	Total (n=543)	Fire (n=181)	Public works (n=181)	Police (n=181)
Great	22%	17%	24%	25%
Some	63	59	66	65
Little or none	15	24	10	11

Note: The respondents were asked: "To what extent have the above groups affected policy in your policy area?" The groups are listed in Table 10.2.

Percentages do not always total 100% due to rounding.

council have far more influence over their departmental programs and objectives than do interest groups. When these respondents were asked to rank interest groups, the chief executive, and the city council as to their relative influence on their departmental programs and objectives, only 8 percent ranked interest groups as more influential than both of the elected positions, and another 12 percent ranked interest groups ahead of one of the elected institutions. However, as we shall note, the influence of interest groups is often directed through the council and the chief executive. Furthermore, that 20 percent of the respondents ranked interest groups ahead of at least one of the two policy-making institutions (the council and the chief executive) is quite significant.

The literature concerning urban politics has pointed to the influence of one interest group in particular, the business community.[11] However, as indicated in Table 10.2, neighborhood interest groups are the most often cited group in terms of influence. A survey conducted ten years earlier is not likely to have produced this finding. The rise of neighborhood groups to such a place of prominence is a rather recent phenomenon. Historically, these groups have sought to protect property values within neighborhoods and to preserve neighborhood life style. In part, their development can be viewed as a reaction to governmental policy. They have always had a keen interest in the zoning policy of local governments. Federal and state programs such as interstate highways that threaten neighborhoods have also encouraged their development. At the same time, federal programs promoting community participation, such as the Housing and Community Development Act of 1974, have stimulated neighborhood associations. None of these factors is as important, however, in the development of neighborhood associations as is the American tradition of localism in urban politics. Neighborhood associations are merely protecting their turf as Americans have so frequently done.[12]

Although neighborhood groups are mentioned more often than any other group as having political influence in

Table 10.2. Most Influential Interest Groups Reported by City Department Heads

Group	Percentage of Department Heads	Correlation of Citing Group as Influential with Indicating Groups Influencing Policy* (gamma)
Neighborhood groups	73	.07
Business associations (Chamber of Commerce, etc.)	50	.21**
Major business leaders (bankers, department store owners, etc.)	48	.24***
Public employee organizations	36	.12
Media	35	.16
Good government groups (League of Women Voters, etc.)	26	.12
Civil rights groups	22	.15
Taxpayer associations	22	.09
Small merchants	20	.18
Real estate associations	11	.22*
Utilities	9	.11
Unions other than public employees	5	.06

Note: The respondents were asked "Which of the following types of groups have had the most influence in your policy area?"

* Correlations are between responses given to this question and those to the question in Table 10.1.

** p < .05

*** p < .01

Probabilities are based on chi square.

cities, the evidence in Table 10.2 makes a convincing case that the business community remains the most influential of interest groups. Note that in the table business groups are divided into four sets — major business leaders, business associations, small merchants, and real estate groups. Half of the respondents cited each of the first two sets of businessmen; next to neighborhood groups they were the most often cited groups in terms of being influential. Of greater importance, the correlations in Table 10.2 between citation of particular groups being influential and of groups in general having influence in policy making suggest that three of the four business groups may be more effective in their efforts to influence policy. The correlation between citing neighborhood groups and general group influence is small and statistically insignificant. Neighborhood groups are probably more numerous than the various types of business groups; but when it comes to influencing policy, business groups appear to predominate. The explanation for the influence of business groups in city politics is thoroughly discussed in the literature.[13]

Readers may be struck by the relative lack of influence of some prominent interest groups. For example, unions and utilities have relatively little influence. These groups tend to be more interested in state and national politics than in local politics. The rates charged by utilities tend to be set by public service commissions at the state level. Labor laws, such as minimum wage rates, are set at the state and national levels.

The failure of public employee groups to be more influential is also interesting. Certainly employee groups have more significance today than they did fifteen years ago. Yet their impact is still confined primarily to management matters rather than policy concerns. If our respondents had been heads of departments where professional values are generally stronger (e.g., welfare, health, or education), the involvement of professional groups in policy might have been reported to be greater. In particular, school boards have complained about the tendency of teachers associations to be concerned not only with compensation and working conditions, the typical terrain of unions, but also with significant policy matters such as curriculum.

Explaining Interest Group Influence

The literature suggests that certain city characteristics might affect the degree or type of interest group influence. For example, political party activity is supposed to discourage such influence.[14] However, our data indicate no relationship between party activity and group influence. Secondly, "reformed" cities are sometimes said to have less interest group activity due to the presence of institutions designed to discourage conflict.[15] Even so, we find that interest groups are perceived to have as much influence in city manager cities as in mayoral cities. Furthermore, reform cities are said to be partial to business groups because reforms decrease access by Democrats and the nonbusiness community.[16] Nonetheless, we find no correlation between influence from business and the use of the city manager form of government. Finally, we might expect to find interest groups more influential in larger cities since such cities might tend to have greater diversity of interests and perhaps more interest group activity and conflict.[17] Also, smaller cities might have a high degree of volunteerism among the elected city officials,[18] and this might discourage interest group influence. As seen in Table 10.3, interest groups do tend to have more influence in the largest cities, but the relationship between size and influence is weak.

Thus, characteristics of cities are not strongly related to our measure of interest group influence. More relevant to explaining such influence are the routes of interest group access to policy and its administration. Because cities have three sets of decision makers, (city council, chief executive, and administrators) groups have three access points to city policies. To measure the significance of interest group influence with the council and with the

Table 10.3. Extent of Interest Group Effects on Policy as Reported by City Department Heads According to City Size

	Percentage of Department Heads			
	50,000– 99,999 (n=300)	100,000– 249,999 (n=141)	250,000– 499,999 (n=51)	500,000+ (n=41)
Extent of Effect				
Great	19%	26%	22%	34%
Some	65	62	65	51
Little or none	16	12	14	15

Note: Respondents were asked: "To what extent have the above groups affected policy in your policy area?" The groups are listed in Table 10.2.

Percentages do not always total 100% due to rounding.

chief executive, we asked the respondents to indicate if such access gave groups influence on policy in their own areas.[19] Forty-two percent of the respondents noted that the ability of a group to influence the chief executive led to the group's influence in their policy areas, and 70 percent indicated that groups' influence on the city council had an impact on policy. The council is apparently under more influence from interest groups than is the chief executive. The study also included a measure of group access to administrators. Each respondent was asked to indicate the degree of interaction between his department and interest groups. Twenty-nine percent of the respondents indicated that there is a great deal of interaction, 62 percent said some interaction occurred while 9 percent claimed minimal to no interaction. Of course, access or interaction does not necessarily influence policy. However, as we shall note below, interaction and groups' influence on policy are related.

The route of access tends to vary by department. As indicated in Table 10.4, heads of public works agencies were more likely than other department heads to cite influence with the city council as leading to interest group impact on policy. Public works decisions have a strong patronage dimension to them, perhaps leading to more council involvement in this policy area. Respondents from police agencies were more likely than other agency heads to cite their active interaction with interest groups. The direct mutual interdependence of police and interest groups is quite high.

Other factors also affect the access routes. Many students of urban government would agree that one of the goals of the municipal reform movement was to reduce the influence of interest groups, especially neighborhood and ward interests.[20] However, as indicated in Table 10.4 interest groups are able to achieve access to urban policy makers through three separate avenues. Have the reforms been totally unsuccessful in reducing the access of interest groups? The answer must be qualified in that the reforms have apparently reduced access in some respects, but not in all.

Table 10.4. Interest Group Routes of Access Reported by Various City Department Heads

	Percentage of Department Heads		
	Fire *(n = 181)*	*Public Works* *(n = 181)*	*Police* *(n = 181)*
Routes			
Chief executive	37%	45%	44%
City council	63	83	64
Department	24	23	39

Note: Different questions are used to derive the percentages of the first two routes and those of the third. Thus, differences in percentages between the first two routes and the third are of no relative significance. The question used for the first two routes asked: "Which of the following are most important in affecting the influence of groups in your policy area?" Nine choices were given, including "their ability to influence the chief executive" and "their ability to influence the city council." The percentages for the third route are based on: "What do you believe should be the appropriate relationship between your agency and interest groups?"

The municipal reform movement sought to depoliticize the urban chief executive through the use of the professional city manager. Mayors are elected and therefore must build electoral coalitions by catering to interest groups. The city manager was to be chosen by a nonpartisan city council rather than by the electorate. The city manager was to be an administrator and not a politician. Presumably, interest groups would have less influence on decisions through the chief executive in manager cities than in mayoral cities.[21] In fact, the evidence supports this assumption. Thirty-five percent of the department heads from manager cities (n=314) perceived interest group influence taking place through the chief executive, compared to 51 percent of those administrators from mayoral cities (n=194). The lesson from these data is not only the difference between the two forms of government in the route of interest group influence, but also that managers are not immune from interest group influence. City managers have often sought to influence policy, and in this political role they surely must be concerned with getting interest group support. Furthermore, the implementation of public policy requires the support of interest groups.[22] In exchange for their support, interest groups probably expect cooperation from the city manager.

Interest groups are not necessarily less active in city manager cities. In fact, they tend to gain access through the city councils in these cities more often than they do in mayoral cities. Seventy-four percent of the department heads from city manager cities (n=314) noted that interest groups gain influence through the city council, compared to 66 percent of the respondents from mayoral cities (n=194).

The major reform aimed at reducing the influence of interest groups upon the city council was the substitution of at-large elections for elections by ward or district. The reformers felt that ward elections made council members perceive issues from the perspective of their district's interests rather than from those of the whole city. Thus through at-large representation, the public interest would prevail over narrower concerns of local interest groups. On the basis of our data, interest groups are just as able to influence policy through city councils where at-large elections are used as they are in cities with ward elections. In fact, the same percentage of the administrators from cities using at-large elections reported interest group influence through the council as those from cities with both at-large and ward elections (72%) and only 64 percent of those from cities with ward elections reported such influence.

The reader may suspect that the result of changing the method of election served not to reduce interest group influence, but instead to change the relative influence of different groups. For example, it might be that neighborhood groups would have greater influence in councils elected on a district basis than in a council elected by an at-large method. However, our data do not indicate that any particular type of group benefited from a particular method of election.

As the municipal reform movement sought to depoliticize the chief executive and the city council, so it sought to ensure administration on the basis of merit rather than patronage. Administrative decisions were to be based not on the interests of the group in favor but on the basis of professional standards and general merit. One of the reforms designed to encourage this development was the use of the merit system of personnel selection and management. Employees would not owe their positions to any interest group but solely to their qualifications to do the specific job. However, the data in this study do not indicate that departments having the larger percentages of their employees on merit systems are less likely to interact with interest groups than are other agencies. Furthermore, the data do not indicate that interest groups have less impact than the chief executive and the city council on agencies with significant percentages of merit employees compared to departments with smaller percentages.

Our data indicate the routes by which groups gain access and influence in city policy making. Which route leads to the greatest influence? As shown in Table 10.5, compared to influence through the chief executive or city council, interaction with the departments is more strongly correlated with the perceived degree to which groups have influenced policy. The correlation between influence and interaction is particularly strong for public works departments. We have noted that the heads of public works departments perceive groups as actively gaining influence through the city council. However, only where groups gain access to the public works departments are they perceived to affect significantly policy in the area of public works. Two explanations for this finding can be offered. First, the measure of influence is based on the perceptions of department heads. Those heads who interact with groups may be more likely to perceive influence than other heads, although the degree of influence may be the same. Where groups establish their influence through the city council or the chief executive, the degree of influence of interest groups on policy may not be so clear. Second, the large degree of discretion possessed by administrators may mean that influence by interest groups is truly through interaction with departments. Our respondents indicated that their department has much flexibility in regard to service delivery (74 percent said they have total or a great deal of discretion) and rule enforcement (70 percent said they have total or a great deal of discretion). We believe both of these explanations to be partially valid. Indeed, we can offer evidence to support the latter explanation.

Interest groups appear to be attracted to agencies possessing policy discretion. That is, groups interact with departments that report significant discretion. For example, of the departments reporting a great deal of interaction with groups (n = 133), 47 percent cited having total discretion in regard to decisions about service delivery (which areas of the city get what services), compared to 33 percent of the other respondents (n = 334). Similarly, of those respondents having a great deal of interaction with groups (n = 145), 43 percent reported having total discretion in rule enforcement compared to 24 percent of the other respondents (n = 356).

Table 10.5. Correlations between City Interest Group Routes of Access and Influence of Interest Groups Reported by Various City Department Heads

	Route		
	Chief executive	*City council*	*Department*
Department Head			
All	.05	.23*	.43*
Fire	.11	.36*	.29*
Public works	.00	.02	.62*
Police	.00	.18	.39*

Note: See footnote on Table 10.4 for questions used to determine route of influence.

*p < .01

Probabilities are based on chi square.

That groups appear to be attracted to the locus of decision-making power is further suggested by a comparison in discretion between two other types of respondents. The first category (n = 115) includes those reporting only some, little, or no interaction with interest groups while also noting that interest groups influence policy through both the chief executive and the city council. The second type of respondents did not report influence through both the council and the chief executive; furthermore, they indicated a great deal of departmental interaction with groups. The second category (n = 80) reported more departmental discretion in decisions about service delivery and rule enforcement than the first group. Where discretion is not delegated to agencies, interest groups focus on the city council and the chief executive. Where discretion is delegated, groups concentrate on the departments. In particular, 27 percent of the first category reported having total discretion in regard to service delivery, compared to 50 percent of those respondents in the second category. A similar difference exists in regard to discretion in rule enforcement. Again, interest groups appear to seek out those departments most capable of helping them.

Interest groups appear also attracted to other actors who exercise power. A chief executive or a city council vigorous in the use of power will attract interest group attention. For example, of those respondents indicating the chief executive rewards them for supporting his requests (n=190), 54 percent noted that interest groups influence policy through the chief executive; only 35 percent of the other respondents (n=353) noted such influence. Of those respondents noting that city council members reward their department for responsiveness to constituent complaints (n=357), 83 percent noted that groups influence policy through the council. Altogether, 58 percent of the other respondents (n=286) indicated that interest groups influence policy through the city council. Groups go to the access point where decisions are affected.

Where interest groups are influential, no single access point exists. That is, those respondents who cite group access at one point are quite likely to cite access at another point as well. Of those respondents citing influence of interest groups on the city council (n=380), 50 percent also indicated that groups gain influence through the chief executive. Only 22 percent of the other respondents indicated groups gaining influence through the chief executive.

Consequences of Interest Group Access

The route of interest group access to city policy makers has consequences in three ways for city departments: in decision making within the department, in departmental relations with the city council, and in relations between the department and the chief executive. Reformers seeking to professionalize administration have on the whole looked at interest groups skeptically; such groups have been viewed as a threat to administrative neutrality in decision making. Nevertheless, while seeking neutrality, reformers have recognized that executive branch departments need the cooperation of interest groups in program implementation. Agencies often find it necessary to go beyond simple interaction with groups in regard to program implementation; that is, groups are also viewed as allies (or sometimes enemies) to be used (or contended with) in departmental relations with the legislative branch and with the chief executive. Whether we are talking about decisions internal to an agency or about liaison with the city chief executive or council, our respondents viewed groups more as allies than as enemies, and their actions in general were perceived as benign. Furthermore, the heads of agencies having direct interaction with groups viewed the consequences of group influence far more positively than the heads of agencies that experienced interest group influence indirectly through the chief executive or the city council.

For many students of public administration the greatest danger stemming from interest group activity is its effect on the impartiality of administrative decision making.[23] A small but significant number of our respondents (18 percent) said that interest group activity tended to discourage impartiality of rule application. The threat to impartiality is most common when interest groups influence policy making through their accessibility to the city council. In fact, the gamma correlation between departmental heads' levels of interaction with interest groups and citing them as a threat to impartiality is a negative .16, while the correlation between their influence through the city council and their threat to impartiality is a positive .63.

A major area of agency decision making deals with how and where to deliver services and which rules to enforce. Department heads claim considerable discretion in regard to these matters. For example, as noted earlier, 74 percent of the respondents reported having total or a great deal of discretion in regard to service delivery. The literature on the politics of service delivery indicates that for the most part municipal government agencies are able to use objective, professional, rational criteria in making such decisions. Thus, while such decisions may reward some groups more than others, they tend not to be based on favoritism, the political strength of groups or political parties, or pressure from external officials.[24]

Our data generally support these findings. Sixty-seven percent of our respondents indicated making service delivery and rule enforcement decisions on the basis of professional standards, and 78 percent on the basis of objective needs. Like most people, administrators also tend to continue to do that which has worked in the past: 42 percent cited this form of incrementalism (doing what worked before) in their decision making. The impact of the positions of the city council (cited by 19 percent) and of the chief executive (cited by 27 percent) were less important. However, where interest groups influence policy through these external actors, agency decisions are significantly shaped by the positions of the council and the chief executive. For example of those administrators noting that groups influence policy through the city council (n = 380), 24 percent noted the position of the council to be relevant in their decisions about service delivery, compared to 9 percent of the other respondents (n = 163). Of those respondents noting that groups influence policy through the chief executive (n = 226), 39 percent noted the position of the chief executive to be important in their decisions about service delivery, compared to 19 percent of the other respondents (n = 316).

The ability of departments to gain influence with the chief executive and the city council is also affected by the route of access. Overall, interest groups are viewed positively in terms of helping departments with the council and with the chief executive. Thirty-seven percent of the respondents indicated that interest groups aid them in the passage of their departmental proposals before the council while only 9 percent said groups hamper the passage of their proposals. Similarly, 30 percent of the respondents indicated that groups tend to support them with the chief executive, while only 8 percent noted that groups weaken departmental relations with the chief executive.

When interest groups have influence with the city council or with the chief executive and at the same time maintain a great deal of interaction with departments, then they offer to the departments an opportunity to influence indirectly the chief executive and the council. For example, of those respondents noting a great deal of interaction with groups and citing the influence of groups with the chief executive (n = 60), 45 percent noted that groups aid them with the chief executive, whereas 28 percent of all other respondents noted this. For those respondents (n = 104) indicating a great deal of interaction with interest groups and their gaining influence through the city council, 51 percent said that groups aid them in the passage of departmental proposals before the council. Only 33 percent of all other respondents (n = 439) noted such a benefit.

While departmental ties to interest groups having influence with the city council and the chief executive are advantageous, we should not overlook the problem noted earlier in regard to internal decision making. The absence of close ties with groups when they have influence with the council or chief executive causes problems for departments. One indication of the problem is the extent to which the influence of groups distorts priorities in policy. Forty-five percent of those department heads indicating group influence with both the chief executive and the council and noting less than a great deal of interaction with interest groups (n = 141) reported such distortions. Of those department heads noting a great deal of interaction with groups and group influence through both the chief executive and council (n = 49), 35 percent indicated that such groups lead to distortions. On the whole, groups are considered by department heads to be beneficial, but apparently they are most so in instances where they not only have influence with the council and the chief executive but are also in close contact with the department.

Conclusion

We suggested at the outset that interactions between city government agencies and interest groups operating in the urban political arena can be both functional and dysfunctional. There is nothing in democratic theory, Redford reminds us,[25] that precludes the consideration of interest group interests in public policy decision making — especially when those interests are forced to contend with effective countervailing interests. Interest group politics becomes problematical in a democratic society whenever it results in special advantages for some which are not readily available to others who are similarly situated. The evidence presented in this chapter suggests that city government department heads are more likely to view interest group activity as functional when it is focused directly on the department. Perhaps this is because departments are also able to use their exchanges with interest groups to serve some of their own purposes such as influencing the city council or the chief executive. By contrast, city government department heads tend to view interest group activity as dysfunctional when its influence reaches them by way of the city council. Attempts by the council to represent group interests with city departments tend to be viewed as unfair particularism. It is ironic that city government department heads view city council attempts to influence them as less compatible with the preservation of administrative neutrality than direct interest group actions. Democratic theory posits that representative bodies such as the city council and the chief executive at the local level are the paramount instruments for directing and controlling the administrative branch of government. Yet, it would appear from our data that city department heads prefer to take their chances within the arena of subsystem politics rather than be subjected to city council intervention.

An earlier version of this chapter appeared in *The Western Political Quarterly*, Volume 38, No. 1 (March 1985).

Chapter *11*

A Comparative Analysis of Service Distribution and Rule Enforcement Decisions in Cities

In an often-cited article, Kenneth Mladenka has argued that service delivery has not been used by the political machine in Chicago to reward supporters. Instead, he reports that service distribution policy is keyed to "past decisions, population shifts, technological changes, and reliance upon technical-rational criteria and professional values." As he notes, his case study of Chicago joins other case studies of San Antonio, Houston, Oakland, and Detroit in certifying that bureaucratic rules control distributional outcomes.[1]

In some ways these studies seem reminiscent of the early studies of policy outputs in state government. Those studies using aggregate data persistently suggested that demographic variables rather than political ones explained policy outputs.[2] However, we suspect that many political scientists are as uneasy now as they were then about writing off the influence of political officials in administrative decisions. Despite the mounting evidence, missing links still persist in making the case for the triumph of professionalism in urban administration.

213

First of all, the case is built upon a small number of single-city studies. Missing from the literature is a comparative study of many cities.[3] Second, as Mladenka acknowledges, limiting his study to services (fire and parks) that lack significant administrative discretion may have biased his findings in a manner consistent with the hypothesis of bureaucratic control of distributional outcomes.[4] Third, not all of the studies of administrative–legislative relations conclude that political considerations are unimportant in administrative decision making. In particular, Douglas Arnold's study of such relations at the national level found that although objective criteria were the rule in administrative decision making, influential congressmen on substantive committees and appropriation subcommittees were capable of influencing administrative decisions so as to favor their constituents.[5]

The data reported in this chapter will help provide some of the missing links regarding the criteria used in urban distribution and enforcement decisions. The survey from which the data come is described in Chapter 1. The data are not focused so much on the issue of party advantage or the benefits received by particular interest groups; instead, the concern is with the ability of the chief executive and the city council to interpose their positions into the administrative decision-making process.

Respondents were asked to indicate, from a list provided them, those factors affecting their decisions about service delivery and rule enforcement. The responses to this question, shown in Table 11.1, provide significant support for the findings of previous studies. Objective criteria, professional values, and past ways of doing things stand out as the most significant factors in influencing decisions. While relatively less important, the positions of the city council and the chief executive are significant. One-quarter of the heads of public works departments reported requests from council members to be important, and one-third of these respondents indicated the position of the chief executive to be important. Altogether 27 percent of all respondents cited the position of the chief

Table 11.1. Percentages of City Department Heads Citing Factors Important in Decisions about Service Distribution and Regulatory Enforcement

		Department		
	All (n=543)	*Fire* (n=181)	*Public Works* (n=181)	*Police* (n=181)
Policy positions of chief executive	27%	22%	34%	25%
Requests from city council members	19	12	26	21
Objective measures of need	78	76	74	85
Professional standards	67	70	63	67
Previous experience with what works	48	42	45	56

Note: Respondents were provided a list including these factors to check those of "most importance in your decisions about patterns of service delivery and enforcement of regulations."

executive, and 19 percent cited requests from council members, as being important in service delivery and rule enforcement decisions.

While the positions of the city council and chief executive may in many instances pose no significant threat to the use of objective, professional criteria, our data suggest that this is not always the case. Respondents citing the influence of the chief executive and/or the council as factors affecting their distributional and enforcement decisions note different effects from the council and the chief executive upon their department than are noted by respondents not citing these external influences.

Considering first those respondents citing the positions of the city chief executive as a factor in affecting their service distribution and rule enforcement decisions, we find that 47 percent reported having been called upon by the chief executive in the year prior to the survey to affect department service delivery patterns, and 27 percent to affect rule enforcement. Altogether, 68 percent of these respondents were contacted by the chief executive about either service delivery or rule enforcement matters. Consideration of the chief executive's position occurs in part, therefore, because the executive seeks such influence.

Requests by the chief executive to department heads do not appear to be politically neutral. For example, of those respondents citing the chief executive's position as a factor in their decision making (n = 146), 23 percent indicated that the chief executive's support for their department was affected by his political philosophy. In contrast, of those respondents not citing the chief executive's position as a factor in their decision making (n = 397), only 11 percent indicated that the chief executive's support for their department was affected by his political philosophy.[6] Furthermore, 33 percent of those respondents citing the importance of the chief executive's position claimed that his support was based on interest group support for their department. Only 19 percent of those respondents not citing the importance of the chief executive's position thought that his support for their departments was based on interest group support for the department.

In essence, in cities where department heads perceived the need to consider the position of the chief executive as they make their service distribution and regulatory decisions, that executive office appears to be more political. Indeed, 60 percent of the respondents citing the importance of the chief executive's position noted that interest groups influence policy through the chief executive in their city; only 35 percent of the other respondents found interest groups influencing policy in this manner.

Just as the likelihood that department heads will consider the positions of the chief executive in making their decisions appears to vary according to political context, so too does the likelihood that department heads will take into account requests from city council members. Of those respondents citing such requests as important in their considerations of service distribution and rule enforcement (n = 106), 64 percent reported receiving in the year prior to the survey calls from council members seeking services or projects for their districts; only 43 percent of the respondents (n = 437) not citing requests from council members as important reported receiving such calls. Furthermore, such calls do appear to threaten the priorities of departments. Of those respondents reporting that they consider requests from council members in their own departmental decision making, 41 percent said calls from council members on behalf of constituents resulted in decisions distorting their department's priorities; 25 percent of the respondents not citing requests from council members as important said such distortions occur. Twenty percent of those who considered requests from council members as important noted that the city council rewards them for providing services to the districts of particular council members, compared to a similar claim by only 10 percent of the other respondents.

City councils in those cities where department heads consider requests from council members in making service distribution and rule enforcement decisions also appear to be conduits for interest groups. Of those respondents citing the importance of requests from council members to their own decision making (n=106), 85 percent noted that interest groups influence policy through the city council; 66 percent of the other respondents (n=437) so described their influence. Of those respondents citing the importance of requests from council members in their decision making, 46 percent noted that the influence of interest groups in their policy area tended to distort priorities; for the other respondents such distortion was cited by only 32 percent.

Our findings reported earlier confirm those of previous studies on the importance for city administrators of objective and professional criteria in their decision making. However, our findings also suggest that for a significant minority of department heads the views of external officials are important, and the positions of these other political actors are not politically neutral in their effects on departmental decisions. Who are the bureaucrats most likely to be affected by these external actors?

Mladenka's study of Chicago suggests we should not necessarily expect to find agencies affected by external actors in cities where political parties are active. Our data tend to confirm his observations. Using the our respondents' reports to determine the level of political party activity, we find little relationship between level of party activity and the likelihood that department heads will take into account the positions of the chief executive or of the council in their distribution and enforcement decisions.

Can we conclude then, as does Mladenka, that service distribution decisions tend not to be affected by elected officials irrespective of city government type, i.e., reform or machine?[7] Our examination of institutional factors such as form of government or the use of at-large elections indicates that such factors have little effect on the likelihood that department heads will consider the position of the council or of the chief executive in making these decisions. Thus, the evidence again tends to confirm the position of Mladenka. However, we cannot give complete support to his conclusion. In Chapter 9, we noted that the nature of council members' intervention in the decisions of city administrators tends to vary by the extent of reform institutions in city government. In cities having nonreform institutions, calls to administrators by council members tend to be more oriented toward procuring favors for constituents.

The likelihood that city government department heads will consider requests from council members and the positions of the chief executive in making their service distribution and rule enforcement decisions appears to be related to their city's political culture. Those department heads who consider the position of the chief executive in their decisions are also the ones most likely to report taking into account requests from council members. That is, 67 percent of those considering requests from council members reported also considering the position of the chief executive; only 17 percent of the other respondents considered the concerns of the chief executive. Interest groups also appear more active in the cities where officeholders affect decision making. Of those respondents considering either requests from council members or from the chief executive during decision making (n = 177), 32 percent noted that interest groups have a great deal of influence on policy in their cities. By comparison, only 17 percent of the other respondents (n = 354) noted such a degree of influence by interest groups. Thus, it appears that an environment of political competition over policy encourages administrative decision makers to pay more attention to the views of elected decision makers.

As we have seen, administrative decisions in city departments appear to be based primarily on neutral criteria.[8] However, those decisions are not immune from intervention by external actors. Neutral criteria are at times affected by factors external to the bureaucracy, and the degree to which this happens appears to vary by political culture. In part because case studies often suppress differences in political culture, the literature has failed to reflect adequately the effects of external actors on administrative decision making.

Although decisions about service delivery made by department heads are largely neutral, major decisions about what services are provided and who gets them are not made by administrators. They do not decide which programs get funded or the fiscal capability of a city to deliver services. Indeed, some studies indicate that the capability even of elected officials to make such decisions is questionable. For example, Paul Peterson notes that elected officials are discouraged from providing redistributive services for the poor because such activities will attract poor citizens and drive out taxpayers.[9] For Richard Rich, neutrality in service delivery by administrators does not overcome the biases of political structures.[10] In that major differences exist among cities in their fiscal capabilities and in their socioeconomic and racial characteristics, fragmentation of governance at the local level does cause disparities in service delivery.

An earlier version of this chapter appeared in *The Journal of Politics*, Volume 44, No. 1 (February 1982).

Chapter *12*

Conclusion

Politics and Administration: Healthy Tension

Throughout this book there has been a recurring theme. State agency and city department heads function in both a political and an administrative environment. The major characteristics of their political environment are elected executive and legislative officials who pursue programs which contribute to their own election efforts, interest group activity which seeks to influence the policy decisions of elected as well as administrative officials, and separation of powers which often results in conflict between the legislative and executive branches of government. It is an environment of pluralist politics. The major characteristics of their administrative environment are neutral competence which seeks to staff government agencies with individuals who are technically competent to perform their tasks and protected during the performance of their duties from the intrusion of partisan politics, professionalism which brings individuals to government agencies who have acquired a skill or level of expertise (often through formalized training) which is of value to the agency and its mission, and a commitment to the values of efficiency in the performance of agency activities and rationality in agency decision making. It is an environment of bureaucratic organization. In each of the preceding chapters the tension between the political and administrative environments of state and city agency heads has been evident. In this concluding chapter we add a normative note to what has up to this point been an empirical study of the politics of state and city administration. The tension between politics and administration is healthy in a democracy. Yet, we believe there is room for improvement on both sides of the relationship.

Neutral competence is a value which state agency and city department heads in the United States perceive to be well established in their respective governments. Our research has found that while state and city administrators from time to time are called upon to provide favors for elected officials, they do not regard those actions to be particularly damaging to the principle of neutral competence. Certainly some administrators would argue that the costs of political intervention are always too high; but as we reported in our discussion of city council intervention in municipal administration, administrators may also be able to use occasions of political intervention for their own advantage. Further, their policy expertise, their alliances with interest groups, and their ability to exercise discretion in policy implementation provide ample possibilities for them to maintain administrative values and protect administrative neutrality.

While we are strongly convinced of the importance of neutral competence in governmental administration, we are equally firm in our belief that administrators must be responsive and accountable to elected officials. However, political control of administration is not without disadvantages. The concept of checks and balances inherent in the principle of separation of powers often makes it difficult for government to act even when experts in agencies of the executive branch recommend action. The bargaining process of pluralist politics sometimes leads to policies with contradictory goals, and fragmented political institutions tend to result in uncoordinated efforts. Yet, administrators can do no more than provide the expertise for good governance; only elected officials can provide its legitimacy. Despite the shortcomings of our representative political institutions, they are essential for the direction and control of state and city administration.

It is clear that elected officials and administrators need each other. Elected officials make government representative and legitimate its policies. They articulate the goals and provide the resources for administrative action. Administrators serve as a source of information for elected officials during the formulation and enactment of policies, and bring their expertise to bear during policy implementation. They may also serve the chief executive and the whole legislature whenever they deter individual legislators from using the administrative process to serve district interests. Yet, while elected officials and administrators need each other, their differing values often lead to tension. Elected officials, reflecting the values of compromise, partisanship and particularism, may change program goals at inopportune moments, not provide sufficient resources for program implementation, and adopt multiple and even incompatible program goals as the result of political compromises. Administrators, reflecting the values of efficiency and professionalism and holding a pejorative view of politics, may confound legislators and the chief executive by their requests for resources, by their expertise, and by their independence. The tension between the two is evidence that neither dominates the other and that each is dependent on the other. The chapters on the influence of the chief executive on city agencies and the governor as chief administrator as well as the chapter on the limits of legislative influence provide ample evidence in support of this point.

It seems apparent that in the interest of good government, both administrators and elected officials need to do their jobs more effectively. On the political side we have learned from our research that in general governors and municipal chief executives are not perceived by their respective agency heads to be effective leaders. State and city chief executives appear to defer to the professionalism of administrators in both policy making and implementation. When these elected officials fail to take responsibility for planning and implementing programs, administrators may be held responsible for program failures that are beyond their legal and fiscal capacity. More importantly, the states and cities where this occurs are deprived of the policy advantages which are normally associated with strong executive leadership. Similarly, state administrators included in our research perceived legislators as failing to understand their programs. Based upon the results of our research, it would appear that political leaders in both the executive and legislative branches must take greater responsibility for coordination, innovation and implementation in state and city government. They have the political resources to make things happen. State and city governance needs the broader policy perspectives of elected officials.

On the administrative side, there may also be room for improvement. According to our respondents, professionalism is an important value in state and city administration. Certainly, inasmuch as professionalism means a more highly trained work force and entails a commitment to the value of neutral competence in administration it is a positive force for state and city governments. However, when professionalism becomes protection of turf, concern for survival, a preoccupation with managerial control rather than program development or an unwillingness to coordinate efforts with other agencies and programs, it is a negative force in government administration. When professionalism becomes an argument against the role of politics in government, it undermines that which makes state and city administration legitimate. State and city governments need the positive aspects of professionalism, not its negative effects.

We began by asserting that government administration is different because of the importance of politics in determining the objectives and maintaining the accountability of administrative actions. The traditional view of the relationship between elected policy makers who possess the authority to govern states and cities and non-elected administrative officials who possess the capacity to influence the manner in which they are governed, is that agencies of the executive branch are made responsive and responsible through the principle of hierarchical authority and legislative oversight of programs. Increasingly, however, it is clear that administrative agencies relying upon their discretion and expertise as well as the institutional weaknesses of the elected branches are able to gain some degree of independence from political leaders. The founding fathers sought to reduce the likelihood of abuse of power by separating the branches of government so that interest would check interest and one branch would be able to check another. Similarly, the tensions in values and the interactions between political officials and administrators may serve to mitigate the abuse of administrative and political authority. In these instances, they should be encouraged as healthy for our democracy.

Notes

Chapter 1.

1. Michael Murray, "Comparing Public and Private Management: An Exploratory Essay," *Public Administration Review*, 35 (1975), pp. 364–71; Hal G. Rainey, Robert W. Backoff and Charles H. Levine, "Comparing Public and Private Organizations," *Public Administration Review*, 36 (1976), pp. 233–44.

2. Herbert Kaufman, "Emerging Conflicts in the Doctrines of Public Administration," *American Political Science Review*, 50 (1956), pp. 1057–73.

3. Paul H. Appleby, *Policy and Administration* (University: University of Alabama Press, 1949); Howard Ball, Dale Krane, and Thomas P. Lauth, *Compromised Compliance: Implementation of the 1965 Voting Rights Act* (Westport, Connecticut: Greenwood Press, 1982).

4. Thad L. Beyle, "The Governor's Formal Powers: A View from the Governor's Chair," *Public Administration Review*, 28 (November/December 1968), pp. 540–45.

5. *The Book of the States 1982–83* (Lexington, Kentucky: Council of State Governments, 1983), pp. 168–69.

6. Francis E. Rourke, *Bureaucracy, Politics, and Public Policy*, second edition (Boston: Little, Brown, 1976), p. 13.

7. Ibid., p.15.

8. Lawrence C. Dodd, and Richard L. Schott, *Congress and the Administrative State* (New York: Wiley, 1979) pp. 291–93.

9. David B. Truman, *The Governmental Process* (New York: Knopf, 1951).

10. J. Leiper Freeman, *The Political Process: Executive Bureau–Legislative Committee Relations* (New York: Random House, 1955); Theodore J.Lowi, *The End of Liberalism: Ideology, Policy and the Crisis of Public Authority* (New York: Norton, 1969).

11. Rourke, *Bureaucracy.*

12. Glenn Abney and Thomas A. Henderson, "Federal and State Impact on Local Governments: A Research Note on the Views of Local Chief Executives," *Administration and Society,* 14 (February 1983), pp. 469–80.

13. George E. Hale, "Federal Courts and the State Budgeting Process," *Administration and Society,* 11 (November 1979), 357–68; and Linda Harriman and Jeffrey D. Straussman, "Do Judges Determine Budget Decisions? Federal Court Decisions in Prison Reform and State Spending for Corrections," *Public Administration Review,* 43 (March/April 1983), 343–51.

14. Lawrence J. Herson, "The Lost World of Municipal Government," *American Political Science Review,* 51 (June 1957), pp. 330–45.

15. Kenneth R. Mladenka, "The Urban Bureaucracy and the Chicago Political Machine: Who Gets What and the Limits to Political Control," *American Political Science Review,* 74 (December 1980), pp. 991–98.

16. Ira Sharkansky in Herbert Jacob and Kenneth N. Vines, eds., *Politics in the American States,* second edition (Boston: Little, Brown, 1971), p. 240.

17. Douglas M. Fox, *Politics of City and State Bureaucracy,* (Pacific Palisades, California: Goodyear, 1974).

18. Malcolm E. Jewell, "The Neglected World of State Politics," *Journal of Politics,* 44 (August 1982), 635–57.

19. The three surveys were supported by research funds provided by Georgia State University. The survey of state administrators was conducted in 1977, the survey of state budget officers was conducted in 1982 and the survey of city department heads was conducted in 1978.

20. *Municipal Year Book 1977* (Washington, D.C.: International City Management Association, 1977), pp. 224–325.

21. In our analysis of both the state and city data, there are some instances where not all respondents answered all of the survey items. This is reflected in analysis based on a sample of less than the return totals reported in this chapter.

Chapter 2.

1. Eugene Bardach, *The Implementation Game* (Cambridge, Massachusetts: MIT Press, 1977).

2. Woodrow Wilson, "The Study of Administration," *Political Science Quarterly*, 2 (June 1887); Frank Goodnow, *Politics and Administration*, (New York: Macmillan, 1900). It is quite likely that Wilson did not intend to suggest that administration could be devoid of conflict, negotiation, and coalition building. Barry Bozeman, *Public Management and the Policy Process* (New York: St. Martins, 1979), p. 31. See also: Paul H. Appleby, *Policy and Administration* (University: University of Alabama Press, 1949); Dwight Waldo, *The Administrative State* (New York: Ronald, 1948); Herbert Simon, *Administrative Behavior* (New York: Free Press, 1947).

3. Joel D. Aberbach and Bert A. Rockman, "Clashing Beliefs within the Executive Branch," *American Political Science Review*, 70 (June 1976), pp. 456–68; Richard L. Cole and David A. Caputo, "Presidential Control of the Senior Civil Service: Assessing the Strategies of the Nixon Years," *American Political Science Review*, 73 (June 1979) pp. 399–413; Ronald Randall, "Presidential Power versus Bureaucratic Intransigence: The Influence of the Nixon Administration on Welfare Policy," *American Political Science Review*, 73 (September 1979), pp. 795–810.

4. Allen Schick, "Congress and the Details of Administration," *Public Administration Review*, 36 (September/October 1976), pp. 516–28; Morris Ogul, *Congress Oversees the Bureaucracy* (Pittsburgh: University of Pittsburgh Press, 1976); Lawrence C. Dodd and Richard L. Schott, *Congress and the Administrative State* (New York: Wiley, 1979).

5. Kenneth R. Mladenka, "The Urban Bureaucracy and the Chicago Political Machine: Who Gets What and the Limits to Political Control," *American Political Science Review*, 74 (December 1980), pp. 991–98.

6. Glenn Abney and Thomas P. Lauth, "A Comparative Analysis of Distributional and Enforcement Decisions in Cities," *Journal of Politics*, 44 (February 1982), pp. 193–200; or Chapter 11.

7. Douglas Arnold, *Congress and the Bureaucracy* (New Haven, Connecticut: Yale University Press, 1979).

8. For example, see Daniel J. Elazar, *American Federalism: A View from the States*, second edition (New York: Crowell, 1972).

9. Joseph A. Schlesinger, "The Politics of the Executive," in Herbert Jacob and Kenneth N. Vines, eds., *Politics in the American States*, second edition (Boston: Little, Brown, 1971), pp. 210–37.

10. For confirmation of this view, see George E. Hale and Marian Lief Palley, "Federal Grants to the States," *Administration and Society*, 11 (May 1979), pp. 3–26.

11. When the respondents were grouped into three categories according to the number of requests their governor had made of them over the course of the previous year, the cross-tabulation between number of requests and the ranking of the gubernatorial and legislative liaison task produced a distribution with a probability of random occurrence of less than .05. Fifty-three percent of those receiving the most requests ranked gubernatorial and legislative liaison as first or second in importance (n = 185) compared to 35 percent of those respondents who reported receiving the fewest requests (n = 131).

12. This interaction with supporters rather than opponents is quite similar to the reported behavior of lobbyists. See Harmon Zeigler and Michael Baer *Lobbying: Interaction and Influence in American State Legislatures* (Belmont, California: Wadsworth, 1969), pp. 128–33.

13. Of those respondents citing gubernatorial and legislative liaison as their primary task (n = 99), only 24 percent indicated having a "great deal of discretion" in how their depart-

ment spent its money, compared to 40 percent of those respondents ranking this task as third, fourth, or last in importance (n = 299).

Chapter 3.

1. Martha Weinberg, *Managing the State* (Cambridge, Massachusetts: MIT Press, 1977).

2. For an application of this concept to the various roles performed by the President of the United States, see Clinton L. Rossiter, *The American Presidency* (New York: New American Library, 1960).

3. Deil S. Wright, "Executive Leadership in State Administration," *Midwest Journal of Political Science*, 11 (February 1967), pp. 1–26.

4. George E. Hale and Marian Lief Palley, "Federal Grants to the States," *Administration and Society*, 11 (May 1979), pp. 3–26.

5. Emmette S. Redford, *Democracy in the Administrative State* (New York: Oxford University Press, 1969), pp. 96–106; J. Leiper Freeman, *The Political Process: Executive Bureau–Legislative Committee Relations* (New York: Random House, 1955); A. Lee Fritschler, *Smoking and Politics: Policymaking and the Federal Bureaucracy* (Englewood Cliffs, New Jersey: Prentice-Hall, 1975); David B. Truman, *The Governmental Process* (New York: Knopf, 1951), especially chap. 14.

6. Eighteen percent of the respondents ranked federal administrators as being more influential than the governor. Similarly, 13 percent ranked interest groups as more influential, 9 percent ranked local administrators, 15 percent ranked the Congress and the President, and 8 percent ranked locally elected officials as more influential.

7. For a discussion of reorganization efforts to strengthen the position of governors as chief administrators see: A. E. Buck, *The Reorganization of State Governments in the United States* (New York: Columbia University Press, 1938), pp. 14–28; York Willbern, ed., *The Fifty States and Their Local Governments* (New York: Knopf, 1967), pp. 337–63; Duane Lockard, ed., "A

Mini-Symposium: The Strong Governorship: Status and Problems," *Public Administration Review,* 36 (January/February 1976), pp. 90–98; David R. Berman, *State and Local Politics,* second edition (Boston, Allyn and Bacon, 1978), pp. 137–44; John J. Harrigan, *Politics and Policy in States and Communities* (Boston: Little, Brown, 1980), pp. 122–25, 155–57. An entire issue of *State Government* (54, 1981) was recently devoted to the topic: see especially Lynn Muchmore, "The Governor as Manager," pp. 71–75; H. Edward Flentje, "The Governor as Manager: A Political Assessment," pp. 76–80; Nelson C. Dometrius, "Some Consequences of State Reform," pp. 93–98.

8. Allen Schick, *Budget Innovation in the States* (Washington, D.C.: The Brookings Institution, 1971), especially chap. 2; "Control Patterns in State Budget Execution," *Public Administration Review,* 24 (June 1964), pp. 97–106, and, "The Road to PPB: The Stages of Budget Reform," *Public Administration Review,* 26 (December 1966), pp. 243–58.

9. State agency heads were asked the following question and were provided the following list of possible answers: "During the past year, which of the following has the governor attempted with regard to your department? Check those applicable. A. To obtain information; B. To encourage coordination with other departments of state government; C. To seek improvements in management efficiency; D. To affect the activity level of your program; E. To use your department to reward his electoral constituents; F. To control your lobbying activities with the legislature; G. To control your relationships with federal officials."

10. See Thomas J. Anton, "Roles and Symbols in the Determinants of State Expenditures," *Midwest Journal of Political Science,* 11 (February 1967), pp. 27–43.

11. Larry Berman, *The Office of Management and Budget and the Presidency, 1921–1979* (Princeton, New Jersey: Princeton University Press, 1979); Richard E. Neustadt, "The Presidency and Legislation: The Growth of Central Clearance," *American Political Science Review,* 48 (September 1954), pp. 641–71, and, "Presidency and Legislation: Planning the President's Program," *American Political Science Review,* 49 (December 1955), pp. 980–1021.

12. Respondents were asked the following question: "How much discretion does your department have in the spending of its funds? A. A great deal; B. Some; C. Relatively little; D. None."

13. Respondents were asked the following question: "Which of the following have been the most important factors in the governor's ability to influence your department's decisions? Check those applicable. A. His prestige; B. His influence on the budget; C. His ability to influence the legislature; D. His ability to appoint and remove; E. Friendship ties between you and the governor."

14. Determined by averaging from each state the respondents' perceptions of the governor's influence on the budget in affecting departmental decisions. See response B in footnote 13.

15. The question was, "Which of the following encouraged these interactions with officials in other policy areas? Check those applicable: A. Personal friendship; B. Mandate from governor's office requiring coordination; C. Federal mandate requiring coordination; D. Professionalism of participants; E. Similar political philosophies; F. Existence of umbrella type organization; G. Physical proximity; and H. State laws mandating coordination."

16. The question was, "In general, when a legislator makes a request on behalf of a constituent, which of the following influence your response? Check those applicable: A. The ability of the legislator to affect your program; B. The legislator's level of previous support for your program; C. The legitimacy of the request; D. The importance attached to the request by the legislator; E. The governor's position."

17. Glenn Abney and Thomas A. Henderson, "An Exchange Model of Intergovernmental Relations: State Legislators and Local Officials," *Social Science Quarterly*, 59 (March 1979), pp. 720–31.

18. Eugene Bardach, *The Implementation Game* (Cambridge, Massachusetts: The MIT Press, 1977).

19. Interaction was defined by the total number of reasons for contacting local administrators, identified from the following question: "For which of the following reasons have you contacted local government administrators in your policy area

during the past year? A. To insure compliance with your regulations; B. To obtain their opinons regarding program objectives; C. To evaluate their programs; D. To obtain aid in gaining the support of a state legislator in regard to your legislative program." Respondents who reported having contacted local administrators with regard to all of these were considered to have had significant interaction.

20. The thrust of legislative reform has been to improve the performance of legislatures through a reduced number of committees, longer tenure for legislators, and more staffing. The result of these reforms has been, we believe, to strengthen committees and their demands on administrators for information.

21. Richard E. Neustadt, *Presidential Power* (New York: Wiley, 1961), p.9.

22. The following question was asked of the respondents: "Which of the following have been important factors in determining the support of the governor for your department? Check those applicable: A. His campaign commitments; B. His political philosophy; C. Your department's achievements; D. The objective needs within your department; E. Your department's efforts to persuade the governor; F. The governor's control over your department; G. Friendship with the governor; and H. Lobbying by interest groups with the governor."

23. Theodore J. Lowi has made a similar point in regard to governance of cities. See "The State of the Cities in the Second Republic," *Urban Affairs Annual Review*, 17 (1979), p. 46.

Chapter 4.

1. Terry Sanford, *Storm over the States* (New York: McGraw-Hill, 1967), pp. 29–31.

2. *The Book of the States, 1980–1981* (Lexington, Kentucky: Council of State Governments, 1980), pp. 196–97.

3. For support of this view, see George E. Hale and Marian Lief Palley, "Federal Grants to the States," *Administration and Society*, 11 (May 1979), pp. 3–26.

4. Respondents were asked to rank seven factors affecting their departments' appropriations from the legislature. Besides

lobbying, the other factors were: state revenue level, governor's position, objective needs within policy area, departmental achievements, interest group activity, and legislators' concern for reelection.

5. *The Sometimes Governments* (Kansas City, Missouri: Citizens Conference on State Legislatures, 1971).

6. Information on staff assistance found in *Book of the States, 1980–1981*, pp. 128–29.

7. The policy areas where departments are most active are insurance, education, consumer protection, higher education, and human services; the policy areas where departments are least active are banking and finance, industry and trade, public service commissions, defense, and corrections.

8. Harmon Zeigler and Michael A. Baer, *Lobbying: Interaction and Influence in American State Legislatures* (Belmont, California: Wadsworth, 1969), pp. 128–33.

9. The administrators were asked the following question: "Which of the following are most characteristic of your department's lobbying of the legislature? A. Lobbying often against bad legislation rather than for legislation you proposed; B. Seeking gubernatorial support; C. Testifying before legislative committees; D. Seeking support of interest groups for your legislative programs; E. Seeking out those legislators with influence; F. Requesting local administrators to contact legislators."

10. Zeigler and Baer, *Lobbying*, pp. 110–68.

11. Impact and understanding were measured separately by asking respondents to rank impact and understanding of legislatures compared to six other external actors. See Tables 2.2 and 2.5 in Chapter 2 for rankings.

12. Jesse Unruh, "The Ombudsman in the States," *The Annals of the American Academy of Political and Social Sciences*, 377 (May 1968), p. 115.

Chapter 5.

1. Francis E. Rourke, *Bureaucracy, Politics, and Public Policy*, second edition (Boston: Little, Brown, 1976).

2. J. Leiper Freeman, *The Political Process: Executive Bureau–Legislative Committee Relations* (New York: Random House, 1955); A. Lee Fritschler, *Smoking and Politics* (Englewood Cliffs, New Jersey: Prentice-Hall, 1975).

3. Harmon Zeigler and Michael Baer, *Lobbying, Interaction and Influence in American State Legislatures* (Belmont, California: Wadsworth, 1969); John C. Wahlke, Heinz Eulau, William Buchanan, and Leroy C. Ferguson, *The Legislative System* (New York: Wiley, 1962).

4. Sidney Waldman, *Foundations of Political Action* (Boston: Little, Brown, 1972).

5. According to David B. Truman, public policy at any moment in time reflects an equilibrium among conflicting interest groups. That equilibrium is established and legitimized by the interaction of interest groups with governmental institutions. Truman's work sought to describe the interaction between interest groups and governmental institutions in establishing public policy. Missing, however, from his work is a theoretical framework which attempts to explain the nature of interest group interactions with governmental institutions. If Truman is correct in asserting that policy conflicts can be viewed as recurring disruptions and restorations of equilibrium, then exchange theory with its emphasis on equilibrium should be an appropriate theoretical framework for explaining interest group–administrator interactions. See Truman, *The Governmental Process* (New York: Knopf, 1951).

6. John E. Chubb, "A Theory of Agency–Interest Group Relations: Policy Impacts and the Energy Lobby," a paper presented at the 1979 Annual Meeting of the American Political Science Association.

7. Peter Blau, *Exchange and Power in Social Life* (New York: Wiley, 1964), p. 101. Exchange theory has proved successful in explaining behavior in a number of contexts, including organizations and intergovernmental relationships. See for example, Stuart M. Schmidt and Thomas A. Kochan, "Interorganizational Relationships: Patterns and Motivations," *Administrative Science Quarterly*, 22 (June 1977), pp. 220–34; Robert H. Salisbury, "An Exchange Theory of Interest Groups," *Midwest Journal of Political Science*, 13 (February 1969), pp. 1–32; Glenn Abney and Thomas A. Henderson, "An Exchange

Model of Intergovernmental Relations: State Legislators and Local Officials," *Social Science Quarterly*, 59 (March 1979), pp. 720–31.

8. B. Guy Peters, *The Politics of Bureaucracy* (New York: Longman, 1978), pp. 137–66; Rourke, *Bureaucracy*, pp. 81–106.

9. The high level of interaction between the environmental protection departments and their interest groups in comparison to the older regulatory departments suggests that the life cycle of agencies begins with frequent exchanges. As the rules and regulations become clearer, the relationship becomes more sedate. The lower level of interaction reported by public service commissions and alcoholic and beverage control commissions support this conclusion.

10. Ira Sharkansky, "The Utility of Elazar's Political Culture: A Research Note," *Polity*, 2 (Fall 1969), pp. 66–83.

11. Daniel J. Elazar, *American Federalism: A View from the States*, second edition (New York: Crowell, 1972), pp. 84–126.

12. See Glendon A. Schubert, Jr., "The 'Public Interest' in Administrative Decision Making: Theorem, Theosophy, or Theory?" *American Political Science Review*, 51 (June 1957), pp. 346–68.

Chapter 6.

1. S. Kenneth Howard, *Changing State Budgeting* (Lexington, Kentucky: Council of State Governments, 1973).

2. Robert Lee and Raymond Staffeldt, "Executive and Legislative Use of Policy Analysis in the State Budgeting Process: Survey Results," *Policy Analysis*, 3 (Summer 1977), pp. 395–405; John Stevens and Robert Lee, "Patterns of Policy Analysis Use for State Governments: A Contingency and Demand Perspective," *Public Administration Review*, 41 (November/December 1981), pp. 636–44.

3. Ira Sharkansky, "Agency Requests, Gubernatorial Support and Budget Success in State Legislatures," *American Political Science Review*, 62 (December 1968), pp. 1220–31, and *The Politics of Taxing and Spending* (Indianapolis: Bobbs-Merrill, 1969).

4. Aaron Wildavsky, *Speaking Truth to Power* (Boston: Little, Brown, 1979).

5. Robert Behn, "Policy Analysis and Policy Politics," *Policy Analysis*, 7 (Spring 1981), pp. 79–88.

6. Allen Schick, "The Road to PPB: The Stages of Budget Reform," *Public Administration Review*, 26 (December 1966), pp. 243–58, "Systems Politics and Systems Budgeting," *Public Administration Review*, 29 (March/April, 1969), pp. 137–51, and *Budget Innovation in the States* (Washington, D.C.: The Brookings Institution, 1971).

7. Allen Schick, "A Death in the Bureaucracy: The Demise of Federal PPB," *Public Administration Review*, 33 (March/April 1973), pp. 146–56.

8. Allen Schick, "The Road from ZBB," *Public Administration Review*, 38 (March/April, 1978), pp. 177–80; Thomas P. Lauth, "Zero-Base Budgeting in Georgia State Government: Myth and Reality," *Public Administration Review*, 38 (September/October 1978), pp. 420–30; Frank Draper and Bernard T. Pitsvada, "ZBB — Looking Back after Ten Years," *Public Administration Review*, 41 (January/February 1981), pp. 76–83.

9. Jeffrey Straussman, "A Typology of Budgetary Environments: Notes on the Prospects for Reform," *Administration and Society*, 11 (August 1979), pp. 216–26.

10. Yet under conditions of fiscal stress the analytical staff necessary to engage in rational decision making may be judged more expendable than line agencies that are meeting program needs and have clientele support. Allen Schick, "Budgetary Adaptations to Resource Scarcity," in Charles Levine and Irene Rubin, eds., *Fiscal Stress and Public Policy* (Beverly Hills, California: Sage, 1980), pp. 113–33.

11. Larry Polivka and Laurey T. Stryker, "Program Evaluation and the Policy Process in State Government," *Public Administration Review*, 43 (May/June 1983), pp. 255–59.

12. Lauth, "Zero-Base Budgeting."

13. Michael Quinn Patton, *Utilization-Focused Evaluation* (Beverly Hills, California: Sage, 1978).

14. Wildavsky, *Speaking Truth To Power*.

15. Where a state did not have a legislative budget office, a questionnare was sent to the chief staff member of the lower house appropriations committee.

16. Frank S. Levy, Arnold J. Meltsner, and Aaron Wildavsky, *Urban Outcomes* (Berkeley and Los Angeles: University of California Press, 1974).

17. Lee Sproull and Patrick Larkey, "Managerial Behavior and Evaluator Effectiveness," in H. C. Schulberg and J. M. Jerrell, eds., *The Evaluator and Management* (Beverly Hills, California: Sage, 1979), pp. 89–104.

18. Glenn Abney and Thomas P. Lauth, "Influence of the Chief Executive on City Line Agencies," *Public Administration Review*, 42 (March/April 1982), pp. 135–43; or Chapter 8.

19. Glenn Abney and Thomas P. Lauth, "The Governor as Chief Administrator," *Public Administration Review*, 43 (January 1983), pp. 40–49; or Chapter 3.

20. The respondents were asked: "How does the governor seek to limit agency lobbying of the legislature in regard to appropriations?" Among the choices offered to the respondents were, "Tries to restrict what agency heads say during testimony" and "Threatens to punish agencies that seek to undermine his budget."

21. Glenn Abney and Thomas P. Lauth, "The Tasks of State Administrators," *American Review of Public Administration*, 16 (Summer/Fall 1982), pp. 171–84; or Chapter 2.

22. However, as Shick pointed out, program budgeting and line–item budgeting are not mutually exclusive. Program budgets are reported by our respondents to predominate in slightly more than half of the states. See Schick, "The Road to PPB."

23. Howard, *Changing State Budgeting.*

24. The executive budget officers were asked: "Rank the following functions in terms of their importance for your office." A. Controlling agency expenditures; B. Providing assistance to agencies to do their work efficiently; C. Serving as policy and planning staff to the governor; D. Providing assistance to agencies to do their work effectively.

25. This indicates the hybridization of budget orientations — the desire to reward program effectiveness coexists with the need to control agency spending. See Schick, *Budget Innovation*, pp. 44–116.

26. Specifically the respondents were asked: "When the governor increases your recommendation, he does so because of: A. interest group lobbying; B. his political philosophy; C. an agency head has convinced him of his agency's need; D. an agency head has convinced him of his agency's effectiveness, E. he seeks to satisfy legislative supporters."

27. This is an interesting finding because the literature on public budgeting has held that governors tend to cut agency requests. Information obtained from our respondents suggest that central budget offices inflict the cuts on behalf of governors, and governors in turn restore some portion of those cuts or add new items to budget office recommendations.

28. Arthur Bolton, "Expanding the Power of State Legislatures," in D. G. Herzberg and Alan Rosenthal, eds., *Strengthening the States* (New York: Doubleday, 1971), pp. 57–74.

29. Charles E. Lindblom, "The Science of 'Muddling Through'," *Public Administration Review*, 19 (1959), pp. 79–88; Aaron Wildavsky, *The Politics of the Budgetary Process*, fourth edition (Boston: Little, Brown, 1984).

30. Clarence N. Stone, "The Implementation of Social Programs," *Journal of Social Issues*, 36 (1980), pp. 13–34.

Chapter 7.

1. "These business, professional, and upper-class groups who dominated municipal reform movements were all involved in the rationalization and systematization of modern life; they wished a form of government which would be more consistent with the objectives inherent in those developments." Samuel P. Hays, "The Politics of Reform in Municipal Government in the Progressive Era," in Harlan Hahn and Charles Levine, eds., *Urban Politics* (New York: Longman, 1980), pp. 57–58.

A rational approach to decision making would include a sequential ordering of the following activities: an explicit statement of long-range goals; the selection of short-range objectives that contribute to achieving long-range goals; investigation of the consequences that would follow from each of the goals and objectives; a systematic search from among alternative means for the best way to achieve goals and objectives; and finally, an evaluation of performance with the intention of modifying means, objectives, or goals (in that order of likelihood). In selecting alternative means to accomplish a given objective, the concept of economic rationality serves as a paradigm. Rationality in an economic sense is aimed at the application of resources at the margin of each program so that the last unit of each good or service purchased yields consumer satisfaction equal to the cost of that unit. For an excellent discussion of marginal utility, see Robert H. Haveman, *Economics of the Public Sector* (New York: Wiley, 1976), esp. ch. 2. It has, however, been argued that rational decision making is in fact irrational; that political rationality (incrementalism and pluralist politics), rather than analysis (economic rationality) produces more satisfactory allocations of resources in a democratic society. See Aaron Wildavsky, *The Politics of the Budgetary Process* (Boston: Little, Brown, 1979), pp. 181–221.

2. Efficiency (i.e., technological efficiency) is the relationship of inputs to outputs usually expressed as a ratio of the amount of work accomplished for an amount of dollars or employee hours expended. Improvements in technological efficiency are achieved when increased output is obtained from the same volume of input, or the same volume of output is obtained from a lower volume of input. Effectiveness (i.e., economic efficiency) is the relationship of inputs to outcomes usually expressed in terms of consumer satisfaction. See Jesse Burkhead and Patrick J. Hennigan, "Productivity Analysis: A Search for Definition and Order," *Public Administration Review*, 38 (January/February 1978): p. 34. Equity in this context is a notion of fairness in the procedures of administration. Rational service delivery does not intentionally benefit one constituent more than another; it is neutral. See Herbert Kaufman, "Emerging Conflicts in the Doctrines of Public Administration," *American Political Science Review*, 50 (December 1956), pp. 1057–73.

3. For a discussion of the caretaker orientation, see Oliver P. Williams and Charles R. Adrian, *Four Cities* (Philadelphia: University of Pennsylvania Press, 1963), pp. 27–28.

4. Robert L. Lineberry and Edmund P. Fowler, "Reformism and Public Policies in American Cities," *American Political Science Review*, 61 (September 1967), pp. 701–16.

5. David R. Morgan and John P. Pelissero, "Urban Policy: Does Political Structure Matter," *American Political Science Review*, 74 (December 1980), pp. 999–1005.

6. William S. Robinson, "Ecological Correlations and the Behavior of Individuals," *American Sociological Review*, 15 (June 1950), pp. 351–57.

7. After noting that "the reformers' goal was to rationalize and democratize city government by the substitution of community oriented leadership," Lineberry and Fowler say that the principal tools used by the reformers to achieve this goal were nonpartisan at-large elections and a council–manager form of government. Lineberry and Fowler, "Reforms and Public Policies," p. 702. In determining the use of nonpartisan and at-large elections, we asked the respondents, "How active are political parties in the politics of your city? A. Very active; B. Active; C. Little activity; D. No activity," and "Which of the following best characterized how councilpersons are elected? A. Council elected at large; B. Council elected from districts or wards; C. Council elected with some members elected at-large and some elected from districts."

8. William Lyons, "Urban Structures and Policy: Reassessing Additive Assumptions of Reform," *Political Methodology*, 4 (1977), pp. 213–26.

9. For a discussion of professionalism and the public service, see Frederick C. Mosher, *Democracy and the Public Service* (New York: Oxford University Press, 1982), pp. 110–42.

10. Glenn Abney and Thomas P. Lauth, "Influence of the Chief Executive on City Line Agencies," *Public Administration Review*, 42 (March/April 1982), pp. 135–43; Eugene Bardach, *The Implementation Game: What Happens after a Bill Becomes a Law* (Cambridge, Massachusetts: MIT Press, 1977).

11. Charles R. Adrian, "Leadership and Decision Making in Manager Cities," *Public Administration Review*, 18 (Summer 1958), pp. 208–13.

12. Edward C. Banfield and James Q. Wilson, *City Politics* (Cambridge, Massachusetts: Harvard University Press, 1963), pp. 153–54.

13. Arnold J. Meltsner, *The Politics of City Revenue* (Berkeley and Los Angeles: University of California Press, 1971).

14. Eugene C. Lee, *The Politics of Nonpartisanship* (Berkeley and Los Angeles: University of California Press, 1960). Also see Oliver P. Williams and Charles Adrian, "The Insulation of Local Politics under the Nonpartisan Ballot," *American Political Science Review*, 53 (December 1959), pp. 1052–63; Chester B. Rogers and Harold D. Arman, "Nonpartisanship and Election to City Office," *Social Science Quarterly*, 51 (March 1971), pp. 941–45; and Banfield and Wilson, *City Politics*, pp. 151–67.

15. Readers surely will wonder about other possible confounding variables. In particular, they may be interested in the fiscal capability of reform and nonreform cities. Our data suggest that the latter are more likely to be among those cities having greater fiscal stress. However, the presence of fiscal stress does not appear related to our dependent variables. This finding is not surprising. Consider attitudes toward efficiency. While fiscal stress may lead to a greater emphasis on efficiency, fiscal shortcomings may result from a lack of emphasis on efficiency. Thus, fiscal stress is not necessarily correlated with emphasis on efficiency. Furthermore, fiscal stress may occur for many reasons other than the attitudes of the city officials.

16. Harlan H. Hahn, "Alternate Paths to Professionalization: The Development of Municipal Personnel," in Charles H. Levine, ed., *Managing Human Resources: A Challenge to Urban Government* (Beverly Hills, California: Sage, 1977), pp. 37–57.

17. Frederick C. Mosher, "The Public Service in the Temporary Society," *Public Administration Review*, 31 (January/February 1971), p. 51.

18. Glenn Abney and Thomas P. Lauth, "A Comparative Analysis of Distributional and Enforcement Decisions in Cities," *Journal of Politics*, 44 (February 1982), pp. 193–200; or Chapter 11.

19. Robert L. Lineberry, *Equality and Urban Policy* (Beverly Hills, California: Sage, 1977).

20. Michael Lipsky, "Street Level Bureaucracy and the Analysis of Urban Reform," in Hahn and Levine, *Urban Politics*, pp. 213–24.

21. Theodore J. Lowi, "Machine Politics — Old and New," *The Public Interest*, 9 (Fall 1967), pp. 83–92.

Chapter 8.

1. Charles R. Adrian and Charles Press, *Governing Urban America*, fifth edition (New York: McGraw-Hill, 1977), pp. 150–205; Russell Ross and Kenneth Millsap, *The Relative Power Position of Mayors in Mayor–Council Cities* (Iowa City: Laboratory for Political Research, University of Iowa, 1971), especially their index of formal administrative power of mayors.

2. John P. Kotter and Paul R. Lawrence, *Mayors in Action* (New York: Wiley, 1974).

3. Line agencies are those which deliver services that are substantive or direct in their contribution to a municipal government's objectives. See Felix A. and Lloyd G. Nigro, *Modern Public Administration*, fifth edition (New York: Harper and Row, 1980), p. 153.

4. George Antunes and Kenneth R. Mladenka, 'The Politics of Local Services and Service Distribution," in Louis H. Massotti and Robert L. Lineberry, eds., *The New Urban Politics* (Cambridge, Massachusetts: Ballinger, 1976), pp. 147–69; Frank S. Levy, Arnold J. Meltsner, and Aaron Wildavsky, *Urban Outcomes* (Berkeley and Los Angeles: University of California Press, 1974).

5. It is not our intention to resurrect the politics–administration dichotomy. Certainly public policy emerges as policy statements such as city council ordinances or executive orders are actually implemented. Nevertheless, in a democratic society it is expected that broad-gauge policy making is the prerogative and responsibility of elected officials (e.g., mayors) or those directly appointed by elected officials (e.g., city managers appointed by city councils).

6. Adrian and Press, *Governing Urban America*, p. 154.

7. Richard E. Neustadt, *Presidential Power* (New York: Wiley, 1980).

8. Martha W. Weinberg, *Managing the State* (Cambridge, Massachusetts: MIT Press, 1977); Kotter and Lawrence, *Mayors in Action.*

9. Twenty-seven percent of the agency heads reported considering the position of the chief executive in such decisions.

10. Forty-seven percent of the agency heads reported receiving requests for services or projects from council members for their districts during the year prior to the survey. In making their decisions, 26 percent of the agency heads reported consulting the policy position of the chief executive.

11. The position of the chief executive was chosen as the most important factor affecting their department's appropriation by a plurality of the agency heads; 43 percent cited the chief executive's position as the most important from a list of seven factors.

12. Forty-six percent of the heads cited such support as important in winning the support of the council.

13. This finding contrasts with the pattern of influence reported in the literature on state government, where most department heads report that the legislature, not the chief executive, has greater impact on their agencies and programs. Deil S. Wright reported in 1967 that a plurality of state agency heads identified the legislature as having more influence on their agency's activities than did the governor. Wright, "Executive Leadership in State Administration," *Midwest Journal of Political Science*, 11 (February 1967), pp. 1-26. However, in a 1974 survey Wright found that a plurality of agency heads viewed the governor as more influential. Wright, unpublished data, American State Administrators Project, Institute for Research in Social Science, University of North Carolina at Chapel Hill, 1976, as cited in George E. Berkley and Douglas M. Fox, *80,000 Governments: The Politics of Subnational America* (Boston: Allyn and Bacon, 1978), p. 101. Data from a survey of state agency heads which we conducted in 1977 support Wright's earlier rather than his later findings.

14. Ronald O. Loveridge, *City Managers in Legislative Politics* (Indianapolis: Bobb-Merrill, 1971).

15. It is a power of the chief executive in 70 percent of the mayor–council cities, but only 3 percent of the mayors in

council–manager cities have veto power. See Adrian and Press, *Governing Urban America*, p. 186, for a comparison of mayoral veto powers among different forms of government.

16. Adrian and Press, *Governing Urban America*, p. 161.

17. City managers do score slightly higher than mayors on the influence index. This appears to be because the former have more influence over the appropriation process, in part because a higher percentage of city managers have the ability to propose a budget.

18. Arnold J. Meltsner, *The Politics of City Revenue* (Berkeley and Los Angeles: University of California Press, 1971).

19. Weinberg, *Managing the State*.

20. Demetrios Caraley, *City Governments and Urban Problems* (Englewood Cliffs, New Jersey: Prentice-Hall, 1977), pp. 202.

21. George E. Hale and Marian Lief Palley, "Federal Grants to the States: Who Governs?" *Administration and Society*, 11 (May 1979), pp. 3–26.

Chapter 9.

1. Herbert Kaufman, "Emerging Conflicts in the Doctrines of Public Administration," *American Political Science Review*, 50 (December 1956), pp. 1057–73.

2. For a discussion of city council intervention in police administration, see Glenn Abney and Thomas P. Lauth, "City Council Intervention in Police Administration," in Fred A. Meyer, Jr., and Ralph Baker, eds., *Determinants of Law-Enforcement Policies* (Lexington, Massachusetts: Heath, 1979).

3. John Harrigan, *Political Change in the Metropolis* (Boston: Little, Brown, 1976), pp. 149–153.

4. This council function has previously been identified by Arthur W. Bromage, *On the City Council* (Ann Arbor, Michigan: Wahr Publishing, 1950), pp. 51–57.

5. Theodore J. Lowi, "American Business, Public Policy, Case Studies, and Political Theory," *World Politics*, 16 (July 1964), pp. 667–715.

6. Emmette S. Redford, *Democracy in the Administrative State* (New York: Oxford University, 1969), pp. 83–96.

7. Forms of government were obtained from the *Municipal Year Book* (Washington, D.C.: International City Management Association, 1977).

8. Edward C. Banfield and James Q. Wilson, *City Politics* (Cambridge, Massachusetts: Harvard University Press, 1963).

9. James Q. Wilson, *Varieties of Police Behavior* (Cambridge, Massachusetts: Harvard University Press, 1968), p. 7

10. Harlan Hahn, "Alternate Paths to Professionalization: The Development of Municipal Personnel," *Urban Affairs Annual Review*, 13 (1977), pp. 37–57.

11. Ronald O. Loveridge, *City Managers in Legislative Politics* (Indianapolis: Bobbs-Merrill, 1971) p. 128.

Chapter 10.

1. Thomas J. Anton, "Power, Pluralism and Local Politics," *Administrative Society Quarterly*, 7 (March 1963), pp. 425–57; Peter Bachrach and Morton S. Baratz, "Two Faces of Power," *American Political Science Review*, 57 (September 1963), pp. 632–42; Robert Dahl, *Who Governs?* (New Haven, Connecticut.: Yale University, 1961); Nelson Polsby, *Community Power and Political Theory* (New Haven, Connecticut: Yale University Press, 1963); and Clarence N. Stone, "Systemic Power in Community Decision Making: A Restatement of Stratification Theory," *American Political Science Review*, 74 (December 1980), pp. 978–90.

2. Betty Zisk, *Local Interest Politics* (Indianapolis: Bobbs-Merrill, 1973).

3. Robert L. Morlan and Leroy C. Hardy. *Politics in California* (Encine, California: Dickenson, 1968)

4. Terry N. Clark, "Community Structure, Decision Making, Budget Expenditures and Urban Renewal in 51 American Communities," in Charles Bonjean, Terry N. Clark and Robert L. Lineberry, eds., *Community Politics* (New York: Free Press, 1971); and Michael D. Grimes, Charles Bonjean, J. Larry

Lyon, and Robert L. Lineberry, "Community Structure and Leadership Arrangements: A Multidimensional Analysis," *American Sociological Review*, 41 (August 1976), pp. 706–25.

5. David J. Greenstone and Paul E. Peterson, "Reformers, Machines and the War on Poverty," in James Q. Wilson, ed., *City Politics and Public Policy* (New York: Wiley, 1968).

6. Alana Northrop and William H. Dutton, "Municipal Reform and Group Influence," *American Journal of Political Science*, 22 (August 1978), pp. 691-711.

7. Theodore J. Lowi, "Machines Politics — Old and New," *The Public Interest*, 9 (Fall 1967), pp. 83–92.

8. J. Leiper Freeman, *The Political Process: Executive Bureau–Legislative Committee Relations* (New York: Random House, 1955).

9. A. Lee Fritschler, *Smoking and Politics* (Englewood Cliffs, New Jersey: Prentice-Hall, 1975).

10. Emmette S. Redford, *Democracy in the Administrative State* (New York: Random House, 1969).

11. Paul E. Peterson, *City Limits* (Chicago: The University of Chicago Press, 1981; Stone, "Systemic Power."

12. Michael N. Danielson, *The Politics of Exclusion* (New York: Columbia University Press, 1976).

13. Stone, "Systemic Power."

14. L. Harmon Zeigler and H. van Dalen, "Interest Groups in State Politics," in Herbert Jacob and Kenneth N. Vines, eds., *Politics in the American States*, 3rd edition, (Boston: Little, Brown, 1976).

15. Lineberry and Fowler, "Reformism and Public Policies."

16. Eugene C. Lee, *The Politics of Nonpartisan Elections* (Berkeley and Los Angeles: University of California, 1960).

17. Zisk, *Local Interest Politics*, pp. 127-34.

18. Kenneth Prewitt, "Political Ambitions, Volunteerism and Electoral Accountability," *American Political Science Review* 64 (March 1970), pp. 5–17.

19. The respondents were asked the following question (percentage distribution of responses shown in parentheses): "Which of the following are most important in affecting the influence of groups in your policy area? A. Their ability to influence the chief influence (42%); B. Their ability to influence the council (70%); C. Their previous support of your programs (18%); D. Their expertise within your policy area (18%); E. Their economic influence (12%); F. The unity of their members (13%); G. The merits of their proposals (59%)."

20. Edward C. Banfield and James Q. Wilson, *City Limits* (Cambridge: Harvard University Press, 1967).

21. However, Northrop and Dutton, "Municipal Reform," argue that the lack of an electoral base makes the city manager more susceptible to group influence than mayors, rather than less.

22. Eugene Bardach, *The Implementation Game: What Happens after a Bill Becomes a Law* (Cambridge: MIT Press, 1977).

23. Herbert Kaufman, "Emerging Conflicts in the Doctrines of Public Administration," *American Political Science Review*, 50 (December 1956), pp. 1057–73.

24. Glenn Abney and Thomas P. Lauth, "A Comparative Analysis of Distributional and Enforcement Decisions in Cities," *Journal of Politics*, 44 (February, 1982), pp. 193–200; Kenneth R. Mladenka, "The Urban Bureaucracy and the Chicago Political Machine: Who Gets What and the Limits to Political Control," *American Political Science Review*, 74 (December 1980), pp. 991–98.

25. Emmette S. Redford, *Democracy in the Administrative State* (New York: Random House, 1964).

Chapter 11.

1. Kenneth R. Mladenka, "The Urban Bureaucracy and the Chicago Political Machine: Who Gets What and the Limits to Political Control," *American Political Science Review*, 74 (December 1980), p. 996.

2. See John H. Fenton and Donald W. Chamberlayne, "The Literature Dealing with the Relationships between Politi-

cal Processes, Socioeconomic Conditions and Public Policies in the American States: A Bibliographical Essay," *Polity*, 1 (Spring 1969), pp. 388–404; Richard E. Dawson and James A. Robinson, "Interparty Competition, Economic Variables, and Welfare Politics in the American States," *Journal of Politics*, 25 (May 1963), pp. 265–89; Thomas R. Dye, *Politics, Economics and the Public: Policy Outcomes in the States* (Chicago: Rand McNally, 1966). However, later researchers did not arrive at the same conclusion regarding the unimportance of political variables in the determination of policy outcomes. See Brian F. Fry and Richard F. Winters, "The Politics of Redistribution," *American Political Science Review*, 64 (June 1970), pp. 508–22, and Bernard Booms and James R. Holldorson, "The Politics of Redistribution: A Reformulation," *American Political Science Review*, 67 (September 1973), 924–33.

2. Although the study of police services conducted by Ostrom and her colleagus in the mid-1970s was based on data from 80 Standard Metropolitan Statistical Areas, that research did not address directly the relative importance of rational-professional as opposed to political criteria in determining the patterns of urban service delivery. See, for example, Roger B. Parks, "Police Patrol in Metropolitan Areas — Implications for Restructuring Police," in Elinor Ostrom, ed., *The Delivery of Urban Services* (Beverly Hills, California: Sage, 1976), pp. 260–83.

4. Mladenka, "Urban Bureaucracy."

5. R. Douglas Arnold, *Congress and the Bureaucracy*, (New Haven, Connecticut: Yale University Press, 1979).

6. The probability of this difference between the two respondent categories occurring by chance is less than one in a hundred, based on chi-square. All other comparisons between respondent categories throughout the remainder of this chapter are also statistically significant at the .01 level.

7. Mladenka, "Urban Bureaucracy," p. 997.

8. Of course, we realize that even neutral criteria have political effects in that even using such criteria some people receive greater allocations than others.

9. Paul Peterson, *City Limits* (Chicago: The University of Chicago Press, 1981).

10. Richard C. Rich, "Distribution of Services: Studying the Products of Urban Policy Making," in Dale Rogers Marshall, ed., *Urban Policy Making* (Beverly Hills, California: Sage, 1979), pp. 237–60.

Index

Aberbach, Joel D., 229n.3
Abney, Glenn, 228n.12, 230n.6, 233n.17, 237n.7, 239n.21, 242n.10, 243n.18, 246n.2, 249n.24
Accountability, 2–4, 37, 39, 154–155, 173–174, 224
Administrative policy making
  council member intervention into, 185, 187–189
  goals of, 21–39, 126–127, 136–137, 210, 213–220
  influence of chief executives in, 154–175, 214–220
  influence of city council in, 214–220
  influence of governor in, 37–38, 47–57
  in reformed and non-reformed cities, 151–152, 219
  interest group involvement, 104, 206–207, 209–211, 219
  limits of, 111, 220
  politics in, 213–220
  rational criteria in, 109–111, 211–220
  state tasks, 28
Administrators
  Backgrounds, 28, 137
  Elected, 5, 9, 18, 44, 49, 96, 159–161
  Loyalty to agency, 159
  Role of, 221–225

Adrian, Charles R., 155, 241n.3, 242n.11, 243n.14, 244n.1, 244n.6, 246n.16
Agencies
  See Departments, City Departments, and State Departments
Alaska, 29
Anton, Thomas J., 247n.1
Antunes, George, 244n.4
Appleby, Paul, 227n.3, 229n.2
Appointment and removal
  city councils, 142–145
  city chief executive, 142–143, 157–163
  governors, 5, 18, 28, 40, 47, 49
  interest groups, 96–97, 143
  municipal reforms, 155
Appropriations
  factors in state appropriations, 30–33
  legislative role, 7, 30–32, 64, 66, 69, 98, 105, 116–121
  past research, 107–108
  rational values in, 106–127
Appropriation committees
  criteria used, 118–120
  influence of, 117
  rational values, 125
Arizona, 148
Arkansas, 29
Arman, Harold D. 243n.14
Arnold, Douglas, 23, 214,

230n.7, 250n.5
At-large elections
    city councils, 141–142
    city managers, 134–135
    council member intervention,
        182
    goals of, 130–132

Bachrach, Peter, 247n.1
Backoff, Robert, 227n.1
Baer, Michael, 230n.12, 235n.8,
    236n.3
Baker v. Carr, 19
Ball, Howard, 227n.3
Banfield, Edward C., 243nn. 12,
    14, 227n.8, 249n.20
Baratz, Morton S., 247n.1
Bardach, Eugene, 21, 233n.18,
    242n.10, 249n.22
Behn, Robert, 238n.5
Berman, David R., 232n.7
Berman, Larry, 232n.11
Berkley, George E., 245n.13
Beyle, Thad L., 227n.4
Blau, Peter, 236n.7
Boards and commissions
    cities, 159–161
    states, 18, 22, 44, 48, 64, 66
Bolton, Arthur, 126, 240n.28
Bonjean, Charles, 247n.4
Booms, Bernard, 250n.1
Bozeman, Barry, 229n.2
Bromage, Arthur, 246n.4
Buchanan, William, 236n.3
Buck, A. E., 231n.7
Budgeting
    city chief executives, 155,
        158–159
    governor, 44–47, 114
    methods of, 107–108
    rational criteria in, 106–109
Budget office
    Executive:
        governor, 112–115
        needs criteria used, 114
        rational criteria used,
            112–114

role in budget process,
    112–114
    Legislative:
        criteria used, 107
        governor, 114
        impact of, 116–117
Bureaucracy, 5, 14, 18, 22, 37,
    153
Burkhead, Jesse, 241n.2

Caputo, David A., 229n.3
Caralay, Demetrios, 246n.20
Chamberlayne, Donald W.,
    249n.2
Checks and balances, 64, 222
Chief executives, 4–12, 21, 22,
    64, 223
Chief executives (city)
    agency relations with,
        168–169, 172–173
    consequences of influence,
        172–173
    federal grants, 175
    formal powers, 154–155,
        157–164, 169–171
    influence index, 156–157
    influence over agencies,
        153–175, 222
    in reformed cities, 143–145
    in weak executive form, 155
    leadership style, 154–155,
        164–169
    policy objectives, 139
    reactor to crises, 165–168
    relative influence, 139, 157
    role of, 222–223
    support of agencies, 145,
        165–167, 171, 173
Chicago, 213, 218
Chubb, John E., 236n.6
Citizens Conference on State
    Legislatures, 69, 235n.5
City administration
    lost world of, 11
    contrast with state
        administration, 173–174
    political environment of, 1–16

City councils
  appropriations, 142–145
  behavior of, 142
  chief executive, 192
  elections, 141–142
  in reformed and non-reformed
    cities, 141, 143
  lobbying of, 143
  rational values, 145–146
  relative influence, 157, 188
  role in administration,
    176–177, 186
  See also Council Member
    Interventions
City departments
  fire, police, and public works,
    14–15, 179–181, 188–189,
    197, 202–203
  in surveys, 14–15
  social service, 175
City managers
  city councils, 158
  city size, 201
  elections and, 134–135
  goals of reformers, 131–132
  interest groups, 201
  mayors, 153, 157, 163–164
  objectives, 155
Civil service, 3, 18, 22, 23, 27,
  176, 205
Clark, Terry N., 247n.4
Cole, Richard L., 229n.3
Colorado, 29
Congress, 25, 44, 82
Constituents and state
  legislators, 8, 13, 46, 49, 50,
  56, 63, 75–78
Council-manager form of
  government, 15
Council member intervention
  agency morale, 185–186, 189
  consequences of, 185–193
  effects on council, 191–192
  ombudsman role, 189
  opportunities for agencies,
    186–190

types of, 179–184, 188
Council of State Governments,
  227n.5, 234n.2

Dahl, Robert, 247n.1
Danielson, Michael N., 248n.12
Dalen, H. van, 248n.14
Dawson, Richard E., 250n.1
Democratic theory, 212, 221–225
Departments
  See City Departments, State
    Departments
Discretion (departmental)
  by departmental type, 180
  chief executives, 15
  in city administration, 139
  influence of city chief
    executives, 172–173
  in spending, 37–38, 45–47, 55
  interest groups, 206–207
  legislatures, 55, 105
  professionalism, 5
  role of, 6
Dodd, Lawrence, 227n.8, 229n.4
Dometrius, Nelson C., 232n.7
Draper, Frank, 238n.8
Dutton, William H., 248n.6,
  249n.21
Dye, Thomas R., 250n.1

Effectiveness and Efficiency
  agency objective, 136
  appropriations, 143
  chief executives, 139, 165
  fiscal attitudes of agencies, 110
  governor, 43–45, 47, 49, 58,
    61, 114–115, 124–125
  legislatures, 120–122, 124–125
  political accountability, 38–39,
    186
  reformed cities, 141
  See also Rational Values
Eisenhower, Dwight, 55
Elazar, Daniel J., 103, 230n.8,
  237n.11

Elected officials
role of, 221–225
accountability to, 2, 4, 19–20,
22, 37, 81
Eulau, Heinz
Executive reform movement
agency coordination, 169
chief executive, 4–5
city councils, 176
council member intervention,
182
goals of, 131, 154
results of, 157, 174
Equity
as an agency objective, 136
chief executives, 139
goal of, 11–12
Exchange theory, 83, 93
Exchange Types
administrator active, 86, 97
interest group active, 86, 96,
104
mutual dependence, 86, 88,
104
mutual independence, 9, 86,
88, 93, 96, 97, 103

Federal administrators and state
agencies, 9, 23–25, 32, 42, 45,
50, 53
Federal funds, 3, 32, 33, 67, 175
Fenton, John, 249n.2
Ferguson, Leroy C., 236n.3
Flentje, H. Edward, 237n.7
Florida, 29, 103
Fowler, Edmund, 133, 242n.4,
248n.15
Fox, Douglas, 14, 245n.13
Freeman, J. Leiper, 196,
228n.10, 230n.5, 236n.2,
248n.9
Fritschler, A. Lee, 196, 230n.5,
236n.2, 248n.9
Fry, Brian, 250n.1

Georgia, 75
Governors
administrative roles, 43–62
budget balancer, 167
chief administrative officer,
40–62
formal powers, 18, 64, 66
political philosophy, 56, 99
relative influence, 25, 111
span of control, 18
weak executive form, 18, 64,
66
Greenstone, David J., 195,
248n.5
Grimes, Michael, 247n.4

Hays, Samuel P., 240n.1
Hahn, Harlan, 151, 243n.16,
247n.10
Hale, George E., 41, 230n.10,
231n.4, 234n.3, 246n.21
Hardy, Leroy C., 247n.3
Harrigan, John, 232n.7, 246n.3
Haveman, Robert H., 241n.1
Hawaii, 77
Henderson, Thomas A., 233n.7,
236n.7
Holldorson, James R., 250n.1
Howard, Kenneth S., 106,
237n.1, 239n.23

Index of gubernatorial
intervention, 98, 100
Index of legislative intervention,
98, 100
Indiana, 29, 30
Interest groups
agencies, 202–203
allies of agencies, 72–73,
103–105, 209–212
appropriations, 143
at-large elections, 204
business, 198

city chief executive, 198, 202–206, 208, 210–211, 216–217
city councils, 198, 202–206, 208, 210–212, 217–218
city managers, 204
culture, 98–103
consequences of group access, 208–211
exchanges with agencies, 21–36, 82–105, 202, 206–207, 212
governor, 41, 42, 45, 46, 53, 100
influence on policy, 197–201
legislature, 72–73, 84, 88, 92, 98, 100, 104, 105
mayors, 204
neighborhood, 198
political parties, 201
public employee groups, 200–201
relative influence, 193, 197–198
resources, 83–86, 90–97
role of, 9–10
routes of access, 201–211
states, 98–103
subsystem politics, 196, 212
understanding of, 72, 73
Interaction index, 98, 100

Jewell, Malcolm, 14
Judiciary, 10–11

Kaufman, Herbert, 3, 227n.2, 241n.2, 246n.1, 249n.23
Kentucky, 29, 53
Kochan, Thomas A., 236n.7
Kotter, John, 244n.2
Krane, Dale, 227n.3

Larkey, Patrick, 239n.17
Lauth, Thomas P., 108, 227n.3, 230n.6, 238nn.8, 12, 239n.19, 242n.10, 243n.18, 246n.2, 249n.24

Lawrence, Paul R., 155, 244n.2
Leadership style
components of, 164–169
formal powers, 169–171
influence of city chief executive, 169–171
Lee, Eugene C., 148, 243n.14. 248n.16
Lee, Robert, 237n.2
Legislative bodies
exchanges with, 7–9
influence over administration, 7–9
Legislatures (state)
administrative tasks, 24–28
influence of, 9, 13, 33, 41, 63–81, 104, 223
liaison of departments with, 25, 27–31, 33, 34, 37, 38
professionalism, 19, 55, 69, 80
role, 18–19
oversight, 22, 100, 225
Levine, Charles H., 227n.1
Levy, Frank S., 239n.16, 244n.4
Lindblom, Charles E., 240n.29
Lineberry, Robert L., 133, 242n.4, 243n.19, 248n.4, 248n.15
Lipsky, Michael, 244n.20
Lobbying by departments
city council, 143, 186–187
council member intervention, 190–191
governor's role in, 46, 55–56, 71–72
legislature, 63, 68–74
Local administrators and state agencies, 9, 25, 36, 42, 45, 52, 73, 74
Lockard, Duane, 231n.7
Loveridge, Ronald O., 245n.13, 247n.11
Lowi, Theodore J., 228n.10, , 234n.23, 244n.21, 246n.5, 248n.7
Lyon, J. Larry, 249n.4
Lyons, William, 242n.8

Management
    council member intervention,
        188–189
    role of governor 40, 44, 45, 47,
        49, 61–62
    versus external relations,
        21–39
Massachusetts, 30, 40
Mayors
    See Chief executive (city)
Meltsner, Arnold J., 239n.16,
    243n.13, 244n.4, 246n.18
Millsaps, Kenneth, 244n.1
Mladenka, Kenneth R., 213, 214,
    218, 219, 227n.1, 230n.5,
    244n.4, 249nn.1, 24, 250n.7
Morgan, David, 133, 242n.5
Morlan, Robert J., 242n.3
Mosher, Frederick C., 242n.9
Muchmore, Lynn, 232n.7
Municipal Reforms
    chief executives, 158
    city council, 141, 176, 185,
        193
    council member intervention,
        182, 184, 194
    effects on attitudes and
        behavior, 147
    effects on policy, 133
    geography, 147–151
    goals of, 130, 132
    interest groups, 203
    minorities, 152
    neutrality, 188, 194
    policy objectives 141
    professionalism, 189
    rational values, 153
Municipal Reform Index, 134
Murray, Michael, 227n.1

Nebraska, 29, 69
Neustadt, Richard E., 155,
    232n.11, 234n.24, 244n.7
Neutrality
    chief executive influence,
        172–173

council member intervention,
    177, 182–185, 188, 193
exchanges with external
    actors, 12–13
interest groups, 88, 196, 209
    212
legislators, 7–8, 10, 63, 64,
    77–79
limitations on, 220
partisanship, 3–4
presence of, 221–222
New Jersey, 29, 30, 103
Nigro, Felix, 244n.3
Nigro, Lloyd, 244n.3
Nonpartisan elections
    at-large elections, 134–135
    city councils, 141–142
    city managers, 134–135
    council member interventions,
        182
    goals of, 130–132
Non-reformed cities
    See Reformed cities
Northrop, Alana, 195, 248n.6,
    249n.21

Ogul, Morris, 229n.4
Ombudsman, 75, 77, 189
Oregon, 29, 103

Palley, Marian Lief, 41, 230n.10,
    231n.4, 234n.3, 246n.21
Particularism
    See neutrality
Patton, Michael Q., 108, 238n.13
Pelissero, John, 133, 242n.5
Pennsylvania, 29
Peters, Guy B., 237n.8
Peterson, Paul E., 195, 248n.5,
    248n.11, 250n.9
Picket-fence federalism, 41
Pitsvada, Bernard T., 238n.8
Political culture, 29, 98–103,
    147–151, 219
Political parties, 22, 29, 39, 136,
    184,

Polivka, Larry, 238n.11
Polsby, Nelson, 247n.1
Press, Charles, 155, 244n.1,
    244n.6, 246n.16
Prewitt, Kenneth, 248n.18
Professionalism
    city chief executive support,
        165
    council member intervention
        185, 193
    effect on responsiveness to
        citizens, 151–152
    role of, 18, 22, 27, 49, 60–61,
        72, 221–223
    triumph of, 56, 165, 213
Public Administration
    comparison with private
        sector, 2–3
    in states and cities, 13–14
    politics and, 3–4, 22, 81, 111,
        131, 190, 221

Rainey, Hal, 227n.1
Randall, Ronald, 229n.3
Rational Values
    administrative policy making
        211–220
    appropriations, 106–127, 145
    city councils, 145–146
    governor, 112–115, 124–126
    interest groups and, 122, 210
    legislatures, 118–126
    municipal reforms, 132, 153
    policy, 22, 121–126
    responsiveness to citizens,
        151–153
    state and city administration,
        13
    value of, 126
    See also Effectiveness and
        efficiency
Redford, Emmett S., 196, 212,
    230n.5, 247n.6, 248n.10,
    249n.25
Reformed Cities (versus non-
    reformed cities)

administrators, 137
appropriations, 143
city chief executives, 139–141
city councils, 142, 192
council member intervention,
    182–184, 191–193
geographical characteristics,
    147–148
interest groups in, 201
minorities, 152–153
objectives of agencies, 135,
    137
responsiveness to citizens,
    151–153
service delivery, 152–153
Reform index, 134, 191
Rich, Richard C., 251n.10
Robinson, James A., 250n.1
Robinson, William S., 242n.6
Rockman, Bert A., 229n.3
Rogers, Chester B., 243n.14
Ross, Russell, 244n.1
Rossiter, Clinton L., 230n.2
Rourke, Francis E., 5, 227n.6,
    235n.1

Salisbury, Robert H., 236n.7
Sanford, Terry, 234n.1
Schick, Allen, 229n.4, 232n.8,
    238nn.7,8, 239n.22, 240n.25
Schlesinger, Joseph, 230n.9
Schmidt, Stuart M., 236n.7
Schott, Richard L., 227n.8,
    229n.4
Schubert, Glendon A., 237n.12
Separation of powers, 64,
    221–222
Services
    delivery of, 12, 213–220
    fiscal attitudes of agencies,
        110, 136–137
Sharkansky, Ira, 14, 103,
    237nn.3, 10
South Carolina, 73
South Dakota, 29

Sproull, Lee, 239n.17
Staffeldt, Raymond, 237n.2
State Administration
    differences with city
        administration, 11–13
    lost world of, 11
    political environment of, 1–16
State departments
    agriculture, 93, 97
    banking, 96
    community affairs, 93
    consumer protection, 71
    corrections, 10, 96
    education, 70, 96, 97
    environmental protection, 96
    fish and game, 93
    higher education, 96
    human resources/services, 29,
        71, 73
    industry and trade, 77
    insurance, 96
    labor, 67
    law, 10, 18, 64, 70, 97
    mental health, 10, 29, 93
    national guard, 28, 67
    natural resources, 96
    public safety, 29
    public service commissions, 93
    state, 70, 97
    transportation, 66
Stevens, John, 237n.2
Stone, Clarence, 126, 240n.30,
    247n.1, 248n.13
Straussman, Jeffrey, 238n.9
Stryker, Laurey, 238n.11
Surveys, 14–16

Tasks of state administration,
    21–39
Truman, David B., 231n.5,
    236n.5, 238n.9
Truman, Harry S., 55

Understanding of external actors,
    33–37, 39
Unruh, Jesse, 235n.12

Veto, 5, 41, 155, 163

Wahlke, John C., 236n.3
Waldman, Sydney, 236n.4
Waldo, Dwight, 229n.2
Washington, 40, 148
Weinberg, Martha, 231n.1,
    245n.8, 246n.16
Wilbern, York, 231n.7
Wildavsky, Aaron, 126, 238nn.4,
    14, 239n.16, 240n.29, 241n.1,
    244n.4, 243n.14
Williams, Oliver P., 241n.3,
    243n.14
Wilson, James Q., 186,
    243nn.12, 14, 247nn.8, 9,
    249n.20
Winters, Richard, 250n.1
Wright, Deil S., 41, 230n.3,
    245n.113

Zeigler, Harmon, 230n.12,
    235n.8, 236n.3, 248n.14
Zisk, Betty, 247n.2, 248n.17